FIRE FIGHTING IN ACTION

JOHN CREIGHTON

FIRE FIGHTING IN ACTION

THE MODERN BRITISH FIRE SERVICE

BLANDFORD PRESS
POOLE · DORSET

First published in the UK 1985
by Blandford Press, Link House,
West Street, Poole, Dorset, BH15, 1LL

Copyright © John Creighton

Distributed in the United States by
Sterling Publishing Co., Inc.,
2 Park Avenue, New York, NY 10016

British Library Cataloguing in Publication Data

ISBN 0 7137 1465 4

Typeset by
Asco Trade Typesetting Ltd., Hong Kong
Printed in Great Britain by R. J. Acford

Contents

Introduction

Firefighting in Britain has undergone some interesting changes since the early times of leather buckets and manual pumps. Organisation, conditions of service, training, vehicles and types of incidents are just a few instances of a new genre of firefighting. Many of the important developments have occurred in the last ten years.

The 1970s and 1980s heralded the approach of new fire engine designs. All-steel cabs became popular along with improved provision for breathing apparatus stowage, while the advent of 13.5 metre ladders saw the gradual demise of Wheeled Escapes, with less than a hundred in use in the mid-1980s. Such neoteric expressions as 'demountable units' and 'pods' crept into the fire service vernacular, while smaller specialist machines like Road Rescue Vehicles and Chemical Incident Units appeared in fleet lists. Latterly, several brigades have expressed an interest in fire appliance manu-

The Wheeled Escape in the background is prepared for use.

facturers normally associated with mainland European brigades while a variety of constraints have brought about the closure of some British companies. The ERF group, for instance, ceased production of fire appliances, but companies like Saxon and Mountain Range entered the manufacturing scene.

Firemen wear full protective clothing as damaged drums of chemicals are unloaded from a lorry on the M6 Motorway.

An increase in provision of breathing apparatus has been one aspect of brigade equipment policies of recent years, the total certified compressed air breathing apparatus held by brigades, being some 12,300, while the days of 'Proto' sets have passed.

A principal event during recent times was the strike of British firemen, commencing at 0900 on 14 November 1977 and ending on 16 January 1978. The strike was called in support of a 30 per cent pay claim, which was based on a report looking at firemen's wages, while the Government insisted on a 10 per cent maximum with a commitment to reduce the working week. Towards the close of the 1970s, the fire service was occupied with thoughts of moving to a 42-hour week which was implemented after various polemics. A short time later, in 1980, fire pay-rise talks broke down when firemen's representatives were informed that, instead of the 18.8 per cent pay increase expected, employers were only going to offer 6 per cent. Following succes-

The colour of helmets was changed from black to yellow in the mid-1970s.

sive discussions, agreement was reached on the 1982 Fire Service Pay Agreement for firemen, leading firemen, sub officers, control staff and non-operational staff, and increased pay rates took effect from 7 November 1983, representing a 7.8 per cent increase. The Officers' Committee of the NJC met in October 1983 and the Union agreed on an increase of 7.8 per cent for Officers.

During the last decade, there have been manifold changes in areas of training and advancement within the fire service. In 1980, the Home Secretary decided that the Fire Services Staff College at Dorking should be amalgamated with the Fire Technical College at Moreton-in-Marsh, the Secretary of State suggesting that this would be a contribution to the savings in Central Government manpower. 1975 witnessed the cancellation of the Accelerated Promotion Course, which had started in the fire service during 1964 following the introduction the previous year of a similar one in the Police Force. In the 1970s, an MSc degree in Fire Safety commenced at Edinburgh University, the award being the first postgraduate degree in the subject anywhere in the world. Recently, there have been changes in the examinations within the fire service; circular No. 6/1976, for instance, suggested that a separate written paper be included in promotional examinations to test the candidate's ability to communicate in writing. Figures for 1979 indicated that the new type of examination for promotion to sub-officer (including objective tests) brought about an increase in the numbers passing: in 1972, only 13.6 per cent passed, but 41.4 per cent passed during 1979.

An interesting development in driving fire vehicles occurred on 3 November 1975 when drivers of fire appliances and other emergency vehicles were allowed to treat a red traffic light signal as if it were a 'Give Way' sign when responding to an emergency call. This provision was contained in Regulation 34 (1) of the Traffic Signs Regulations and General Directions (1975) following the expression of views at the Court of Appeals in February 1971. The Home Office drew attention to the need to employ all audible and visible warning devices and to exercise particular care at red traffic light signals.

Uniform design has altered over the last decade as officers in Warwickshire experimented with 'naval style pullovers' in 1975, which were to replace undress tunics on less formal occasions. The decision to change the colour of firemen's helmets was reached about this time when canary yellow was agreed on by the Central Fire Brigade's Advisory Council (CFBAC) on the advice of the Joint Committee on uniform and personal equipment. Officers' helmets remained white while firemen had their's painted in canary yellow, shade 309, as laid down in BS 301C:1964. The CFBAC also suggested in 1975 that plastic chin straps in use be replaced by leather ones. Old-style double-breasted undress uniform in 771A serge cloth was replaced in 1973 by a single breasted wool/polyester cloth uniform, while the working rig introduced in 1975 took over from the former cotton drill bib and brace overall with jacket. During 1979, the CFBAC recommended the naval style pullover for all ranks, and, more recently, the gaberdine raincoat was replaced by an anorak in several brigades. On the recommendation of the CFBAC, a modified Nomex tunic was approved for the fire service by the Secretary of State, comprising an outer shell and detachable lining, and this revised specifi-

One-piece jackets with reflective strips are worn over fire tunics at road traffic accidents.

cation replaced the one of 1974. The waistcoat-style jacket worn over the tunic at road traffic accidents has gradually been replaced by a full one-piece jacket with reflective strips. Outdoor uniform clothes for firemen were included in a new 1983 British Standard, and BS 6308 'Men's Uniforms' contains a number of interesting ideas: size designations were based on wearer's body measurements and not on garment measurements as was formerly the case. BS 6308 provides for improved flexibility in uniform buying and allows manufacturers to make economies by adopting a common approach to design and sizing. Certain brigades were given a new-style fire tunic in 1983–84 for trial purposes, made mainly from wool, featuring reflective strips at the front, rear and bottom edges.

Amidst the plethora of developments in Britain's fire scene, one immutable factor has been the efficient way in which firefighting is carried out, which has been highlighted by major incidents. During June 1974, the town of Flixborough became a household name following a massive explosion which ripped through a chemical plant, damaging 2,000 buildings within a five-mile radius, and testing the strength of local fire brigades. At 0857 on 28 February 1975, London Fire Brigade received notification of a train which had run into buffers at Moorgate tube station; the Brigade toiled for five days in difficult conditions underground at an incident involving some 1,324

London Fire Brigade personnel. The summer of 1976 will long be remembered as a time when drought conditions increased the number of fire calls to 272,900 small fires, including heathland and grass, compared with about 170,000 the previous Year. The total fire calls during 1976 numbered 393,600, and brigade resources were pushed to the limit with the unprecedented number of fire calls. Major fires increase the country's fire damage and fourteen fires alone cost more than £250,000 each, in 1979. In December 1980, a £12 million shopping precinct fire devastated a Liverpool shopping complex. At the height of the blaze, a total of seven Turntable Ladders and Hydraulic Platforms plus twenty-five Pumping appliances were in use and the Liverpool Salvage Corps spread over one thousand salvage sheets, keeping their appliances in attendance for a continuous period of eighteen days. 1981 will be remembered as the year of rioting which took place during the summer when civil disturbances involving attacks on fire personnel and their appliances highlighted some of the problems faced by firefighters in a modern society. During this year, a serious fire and explosions at Stalybridge made headlines when 200 firemen on thirty-seven appliances tackled a major chemical fire which required 8,615 gallons of foam to contain it. The following year, a huge explosion devastated a Salford warehouse, damaging adjoining properties and causing one thousand residents to be evacuated. The first explosion could be heard up to fourteen miles away and, as firemen fought the conflagration, further explosions took place. Close liaison between fire authorities was observed during the summer of 1983 when a huge oil tank caught fire at Milford Haven, Dyfed. Some 105,000 gallons of foam liquid were despatched to

The desperate struggle to contain the blaze at Stalybridge involved 37 appliances and 200 fire personnel.

Forty-five Pumping Appliances and ten Hydraulic Platforms fight the fire at Milford Haven.

Milford Haven from as far afield as Great Yarmouth and Greater Manchester; at the height of the blaze, forty-five pumps, ten Hydraulic Platforms and thirteen Foam Tenders were in attendance. During 1984, a massive blaze took place in York Minster, the largest Gothic Cathedral in Europe. One hundred and twenty firemen from North Yorkshire and surrounding districts battled to control flames leaping 200 feet into the night air as molten lead and timber fell around them. This £3 million fire was brought under control after a three-hour battle by whole-time and retained firemen.

Fascinating developments in firefighting at sea have been encouraged by the quest for oil around Britain's coasts where outside help is minimal when a fire occurs. A new breed of offshore firefighter vessels includes vessels like *Iolair* and *Seaforth Clansman* whose two twin centrifugal pumps each deliver 18,500 litres of sea water a minute at 15.5 bar. Novel trends encourage the rôle of the helicopter in firefighting operations, the Joint Committee of Fire Brigade Operations having established a study group in 1976 to consider the rôle of light aircraft and helicopters in the fire service. Certain brigades in the 1980s have experimented with helicopters for the transportation of men and for hose laying purposes.

Land-based modes of tackling fires have improved over the years, the 1980s witnessing the introduction of thermal cameras providing fire fighters with through-smoke vision, allowing them to locate the seat of a fire. A thermal imaging camera was used at an incident for the first time in 1983 at London's Hyde Park Hotel. One important feature of the Fire Service in the 1980s is the increased use of microcomputers, several brigades employing them in control systems, while one can also observe microcomputers at work

Hose laying by helicopter in the Highlands and Islands Fire Brigade area, Scotland (formerly Northern Fire Brigade).

A Thermal Imaging Camera is carried by the fireman in the centre as crews prepare to enter a blazing factory.

in fire appliances. On the latest Merryweather Turntable Ladders, the hydraulics are controlled by a microcomputer which determines safety limits, taking into account such factors as extension, angle of elevation and the number of personnel on the ladder.

Whilst undergoing a considerable transition in the last decade, the fire and rescue services of the mid-1980s continue to reflect the reputable tradition, training, dedication and organization of those involved in firefighting in Britain.

1

Historical Perspective

Early Britons made primitive efforts to fight fires, records showing that the Roman occupation of Britain brought with it organised groups of *vigiles* who could be called on to tackle fires. During Anglo-Saxon times and the period of the Danish occupation, small towns were built, the houses closely packed inside palisades which encouraged the spread of fire. The Norman conquest and its attendant laws helped in some ways to combat fire, citizens being requested to extinguish house fires at nightfall with a cover—*couvre feu,* hence the word curfew.

During the 1400s, ordinances were passed whereby people could be fined for lighting house fires beneath wooden chimneys, while the sixteenth century witnessed the inception of primitive efforts to establish a fire fighting force, with places such as Winchester and Bristol requiring house-holders to attend fires with a bucket for the purposes of firefighting.

The first patent to be issued for a fire extinguishing machine was granted to a Roger Jones during 1625 and in his 1634 *Treatise on Art and Nature* John Bate noted the need to provide wheels for engines designed to fight fires. Prior to this, various firefighting devices had been tried, including brass syringes or fire squirts, and a piece of mobile apparatus proved attractive for a number of places including Braintree and Glasgow (1656). Descriptions of fire engines attending a fire are given in the Wallington Journal MS, which provides an account of a fire on London Bridge in 1633 when forty-two houses were destroyed; most engines featured a cistern which had to be filled by bucket chain, and were the type of engine being produced by Wharton, Strode and Keeling in the 1670s. During 1674, Isaac Thompson made an engine for Sir Samuel Morland which was shown to the King, a Robert Ledingham receiving a patent four years later.

Fire engine design moved on quickly when Captain-General Jan van der Heiden of the Amsterdam Fire Brigade invented a new engine, also introducing the leather delivery hose in place of a gooseneck nozzle, enabling a jet to be directed on to the seat of the fire.

The Great Fire of London has been well chronicled. Commencing on 2 September 1666 and burning for four days, it destroyed five-sixths of the city, but it had a number of far reaching consequences—private and voluntary firefighting provisions were established alongside municipal and government efforts, authorities appreciating that brick buildings would be preferable to wooden construction. An Act of 1667 created four areas in the capital, each district possessing leather buckets, ladders and similar firefighting gear. A further consequence of the events of 1666 was the establishment of an office for the insurance of buildings against fire, later referred to as the Fire Office, employing Thames watermen as firemen.

The emblem of the Northern Assurance Company is the Scottish Lion on a yellow field upon a shield surmounted by a crown.

Two fire marks from the eighteenth and nineteenth centuries. The top emblem represents the London and Lancashire Fire Insurance Company. The bottom one is the fire mark of the Salop Fire Office, founded in 1780.

The Fire Office experienced a number of difficulties in the 1680s, including competition from the newly established Friendly Society, and in 1693, the Fire Office started a mutual scheme to compete with the Society. Following this, there was a decline in the affairs of the Fire Office and the company was renamed the Phoenix Office during 1705, the Fire Office issuing marks depicting a phoenix and bearing policy numbers. One instance of an early company was the Salop Fire Office, established in June 1780 to effect insurance from loss and damage by fire in Shropshire and the surrounding counties. Firemen were equipped with manually-pumped fire engines of the Newsham variety, buckets, ladders and hooks. The Northern Assurance Company began in Aberdeen during 1836, merging with the Commercial Assurance Company in 1968.

The London and Lancashire Fire Insurance Company (1861–1961) was initially based in London and Liverpool; the first claim met by the company was for sixteen shillings and sixpence paid out in 1862 following a fire in a London haberdashery shop. More fire insurance companies were formed, employing eight to thirty men in a brigade, dressed in distinctive liveries, whose obligation was to the insurance company that employed them.

During 1721, Richard Newsham was granted a patent for a new water engine for extinguishing fires, ensuing years bringing half a dozen sizes of engine, insurance companies being quick to take advantage. At the start of the nineteenth century, some fifty manual fire engines came into use with various insurance companies' fire brigades in London.

The first steam fire engine was invented in 1829, by John Braithwaite,

Dating from 1882, the Manual Shand Mason Pump was operated by 22 men.

although the manual type of engine continued to be popular until the advent of Shand Mason's steam engine in 1858, from which time the steam fire engine slowly replaced the manual models.

BRAIDWOOD AND SHAW

Following a number of devastating fires in the early 1820s, a group of insurance officers and public figures discussed the possibility of setting up an organized firefighting force called the Edinburgh Fire Engine Establishment (1824). The Edinburgh Brigade is often referred to as the first municipal brigade in the history of the United Kingdom, and its first Firemaster, James Braidwood, headed a force of eighty men, between eighteen and twenty-five years of age. Following his success in Edinburgh, Braidwood was asked to accept the post of Chief Officer for the London Fire Engine Establishment which began in January 1833, comprising eighty paid firemen who manned nineteen fire stations. Braidwood met his end when a wall collapsed and buried him during a six-storey warehouse fire, and Captain Eyre Massey Shaw was appointed as his successor in 1861.

During Shaw's period in office, the Metropolitan Fire Brigade Act of 1865 was passed, placing London firefighting forces under the control of the

Edinburgh's first motorised tender arrived during 1908 with Humber chassis and bodywork from Brigade Workshops.

London authorities, and instituting the Metropolitan Fire Brigade on 1 January 1866, Captain Shaw becoming first Chief Officer. That year saw the start of the London Salvage Corps, with eighteen fire insurance offices becoming founder members. During 1889, the newly-formed London County Council took over control of the Brigade from the Metropolitan Board of Works. Shaw did not agree with the power of this authority, resigning in 1891, and was succeeded by James Sexton Simonds. The same year, the National Fire Brigade's Union issued a standard drill book. The title London Fire Brigade appeared in 1904 when the Chief Fire Officer was Rear Admiral James de Courcy Hamilton.

POLICE BRIGADES

Fire brigade work in the early 1900s, represented by Leicester Fire Brigade. The horse-drawn ambulance was introduced in the 1890s, remaining in use until 1921.

Police brigades were organised as part of the police force, personnel usually carrying out duties of both firemen and policemen. In 1860, a police brigade was established in Leeds, running alongside insurance brigades, while Nottingham had a Superintendent and Inspector plus eight others who were full time firemen aided by about 150 police officers who had monthly fire drills. At the close of the nineteenth century, the Liverpool Brigade comprised a Chief Superintendent who received £370 a year, five Inspectors,

Where Police Brigades were in existence, men were expected to carry out duties of both policemen and firemen.

eleven sergeants and sixty constables. The dual nature of rôles was underlined in Leicester where one George Clamp was appointed Superintendent of the Borough Fire Brigade on 10 April 1864, this man having served with both the London Metropolitan Fire Establishment and the Metropolitan Police Force. In addition to being in charge of Leicester's firefighting force, Clamp was given the rank of Inspector in the Police Force.

Some authorities expected the fire brigade to operate an ambulance service and to provide a horse-drawn vehicle for conveying convicted criminals to jail.

THE EARLY TWENTIETH CENTURY

Fire appliances comprised a variety of types at the start of the 1900s as typified by the Central District of Liverpool in 1900 which had five steamers, one chemical machine, two hose carriages, two escapes and three tenders based at Hatton Garden.

The popularity of self-propelled steamers was axiomatic in the early 1900s as Leyland in Lancashire received the first in 1902, followed by Liverpool, Plymouth, Portsmouth and London. Edinburgh brigade acquired its first motorised fire engine during 1906, a Merryweather Fire King carrying water tanks on each side of the boiler, containing enough water for the engine to run up to forty minutes.

Merryweather 'Fire Kings', each capable of delivering 400 gallons of water a minute.

The outbreak of World War One brought a drop in manning levels among volunteer and retained brigades as personnel joined the armed forces. Wartime firemen had to contend with fires started by bombs dropped by German

Fire brigade work in the early twentieth century, again represented by Leicester Fire Brigade, tackling a fire during 1910.

aircraft, which commenced daylight raids on London in 1916, as well as airship and aircraft night raids, while a conflagration at a Morecambe munitions factory in 1917 required scores of fire appliances from as far afield as Liverpool and Manchester.

As the war drew to a close, the Inaugural Committee of the Institution of Fire Engineers (IFE) was held in Leicester, the first general meeting of the IFE taking place in London in 1919. The Royal Commission on Fire Brigades and Fire Prevention published its findings during August 1923, the salient ones suggesting that systematic arrangements should be made for training officers and firemen, that firemen should be pensioned and paid on the police scale, and that improved co-operation should be seen between brigades, whilst public fire protection ought to be obligatory and not optional.

Shortly after, the Fire Brigades Pension Action provided that a whole-time fireman, who had done twenty-five years' service and reached the age of fifty-five, should be able to retire and receive a pension on half pay. In the 1920s, there was increased interest in Proto breathing apparatus sets at a time when smoke helmets were still in vogue, the wearer being supplied with air by means of a pipeline connected to a set of bellows.

Some interesting suggestions emanated from the 1936 Riverdale Committee on Fire Brigade Services, including one which led to the establishment of approved training schools, and another which opined that a Government inspection should accompany the introduction of an Exchequer grant to ensure the maintenance of proper standards of efficiency.

The Committee gave the number of firemen in principal brigades in

Horse-drawn appliances line up outside Canning Town Fire Station in 1912.

England and Wales in 1936 as 16,564, made up as follows: 2,195 Policemen
who could be called on for fire duty, 4,272 Permanent men, 5,351 Volunteers, and 4,746 Retained men. There also existed works brigades and small
village units. The standard of fire cover in the late 1930s was far from
uniform; for instance, Huddersfield's population of 114,000 relied on a
police brigade of thirteen regulars and fourteen auxiliary policemen, while
Oxford's 81,000 inhabitants were afforded fire cover by forty volunteers.

Local authorities outside London were under no legal obligation to maintain fire brigades, and it was not until the 1938 Fire Brigades Act that 'fire
authorities' were created in Britain (with special provision for the Highland
areas of Scotland) responsible for the supply of a firefighting organisation for
areas under their control.

The 1938 Act never became fully operative owing to the outbreak of war
the following year. At this time, some 1,400 local authority brigades existed
in England and Wales, about 185 in Scotland and twelve or more (excluding
volunteers) in Northern Ireland.

*Fire Station design of the
1930s typified by Strathmore
Avenue Station, Dundee,
opened in 1932.*

WORLD WAR TWO

The move towards war underlined the need to form an Auxiliary Fire
Service (AFS) of volunteers enrolled by fire brigades to take on training in
their spare time. As war started, the AFS numbered about one hundred
thousand personnel, some trained to fight fires after the expected air raids,
others undergoing the sixty hours' training. During 1940, the AFS had
25,000 mobile pumps, 3,000 miles of delivery hose, 80,000 branches and
135,000 nozzles.

The sterling work done by firefighters during the war years is legendary;

*These NFS personnel are
inspecting a bombed factory.*

Built at the start of World War Two, this trailer pump was towed by a vehicle to incidents.

Popular during World War Two, Austin Auxiliary Towing Vehicles were based on the Standard Austin K2.

in the London area alone between the September and December of 1940, there were almost 34,000 calls to incidents caused by enemy action.

The widespread attacks on centres of population pointed to the great diversity in such matters as training, organisation, appliances and equipment, so a unified command with standard operational procedure became a priority. As a consequence of this, and as a wartime measure only, the National Fire Service was formed in 1941 by the amalgamation of the AFS and local brigades into a single organization. Ministerial responsibility for firefighting in England and Wales was vested in the Home Secretary, in Scotland in the Secretary of State for Scotland and in the former Ministry of Home Affairs in Northern Ireland.

The nation now boasted a national scheme of fire defence comprising thirty-nine fire forces instead of some 1,400 fire brigades, and in 1942 the Government decided to increase the weekly minimum wage of non-regular firefighters to seventy-four shillings plus a deferred weekly payment of three shillings and sixpence which put the average firefighter on an income similar to that of a soldier.

THE POSTWAR YEARS

As the war drew to a close, the strength of the NFS was cut to 52,000 in June 1945, and had dropped to 31,000 by the end of the year. Not long after the war, the Government decided on the abolition of the NFS, with responsibility of fire protection returned to local authorities by the 1947 Fire Service Act; a similar restoration of responsibility was effected in Northern Ireland under the provision of the Fire Services Act (Northern Ireland) of 1950.

Two main differences distinguished the postwar from the pre-war services—the smaller number of authorities, plus the element of central control which was maintained. The local authority fire brigades absorbed the principal operational features developed during the time of the NFS.

26

This Dennis F8 major pump was part of the postwar replacement programme, surviving into the Essex Fire Brigade fleet.

Developed from an old limousine pump, the Emergency Tender served with Cambridgeshire Fire Brigade in the early 1950s.

The so-called Cold War of postwar years encouraged the passing of the 1948 Civil Defence Act, and, in 1949, voluntary recruitment commenced with fire authorities seeking two male recruits for every whole time member of the brigade. Central supervision of fire brigades in the 1950s was improved with the establishment of the Central Fire Brigades Advisory Council for England and Wales.

Working conditions changed in the 1950s. The first county brigade to adopt the fifty-six-hour week was Hertfordshire in 1955, while, amid considerable controversy, the Auxiliary Fire Service was disbanded in 1968. Many authorities still had examples of emergency type fire appliances, although pre-war manufacturers slowly resumed production, Dennis introducing their F7 model in 1949 while bodymakers such as Miles, Carmichael and HCB produced coachwork for appliances.

The 1970 Report of the Departmental Committee of the Fire Service concluded that the operational efficiency of the service was satisfactory, that it should stay under local authority control and that recruitment should continue to be based on a one tier entry system.

Under the Local Government Act of 1974, the provision of fire services in England and Wales (outside Greater London) became the responsibility of the administrative counties. The names of long established brigades were altered with re-organisation, this period seeing the end of the smaller fire brigades in the United Kingdom, such as Wakefield and Birkenhead.

The Local Government (Scotland) Act of 1975 provided that some of the counties were combined, resulting in eight fire areas, each with a single brigade. In Northern Ireland, the Fire Authority for Northern Ireland was set up on 1 October 1973.

The first meeting of the Executive's Advisory Committee on Dangerous Substances took place in 1977. It was seen at the time as the principal force to prepare controls over dangerous substances, with a sub committee on the Standing Panel on Dangerous Substances approving arrangements for a survey of chemical incidents to be carried out in 1980. In that year, a consultative document from the Health and Safety Commission introduced controls over the conveyance of dangerous substances by road, by means of three sets of regulations under the Health and Safety at Work Act. The Health and Safety Executive published in 1981 guidance on the Dangerous Substances Regulations which came into force in January 1982 after they were put before Parliament in August the previous year.

THE 1980s

The UK Fire Service's future was outlined in a Government publication, a Green Paper, *Future Fire Policy: A Consultative Document*, a Home Office

Fire Department publication of 1980, based on the Home Office *Review of Fire Policy: An Examination of the Deployment of Resources to Combat Fire*. Among its findings, the Green Paper suggested investigations into whether the frequency or severity of fires in 'A' and 'B' risk areas required the current standard of cover, and examine the definition of 'C' risk areas.

The Green Paper expressed doubts about the working of the Fire Precautions Act, underlining the cost of enforcement of the Act, which was £16.25 million per annum at 1977/78 prices. The Green Paper, commenting on certification of premises, noted that a more selective approach is required for the future, even if it involved fresh legislation.

The Green Paper referred to the cost of fire, stating, among other things, that a high proportion of total property loss (£300 million in 1978) resulted from a very small number of fires; that fires reported to UK brigades amounted to about 300,000 a year; and about 40 percent of large loss fires occurred between 2200 and 0600 hours.

Various fire brigade unions and organisations commented on the Green Paper in 1980, and, at a special meeting in February 1981, the Central Fire Brigade's Advisory Council for England and Wales and for Scotland decided to establish a joint committee to discuss suggestions for changes to the guidance on standards of fire cover and to assess the needs of special, emergency and other services.

The Green Paper noted that fires reported to brigades numbered 300,000 per annum. Here Cambridgeshire firemen tackle a blazing thatched roof.

During 1981, the Joint Fire Prevention Committee proposed legislation replacing music and dancing legislation in England and Wales by a uniform code of licensing, and these, plus other proposals, were included in the Local Government (Miscellaneous Provisions) Bill which was given the Royal Assent on 13 July 1982. This introduced from 1 January 1983, a standard procedure for the licensing of public entertainments in England and Wales (apart from Greater London) and gave fire authorities new powers of inspection.

The Cinematograph (Amendment) Act 1982 came into force on 13 October 1982 and contained similar powers, while new safety standards for exhibition in certain premises were set out in the Cinematograph (Safety) Amendment Regulations 1982.

Among noteworthy occurrences of 1983–84 one can consider the closure of the three UK Salvage Corps at London, Glasgow and Liverpool, thus ending a tradition of firefighting and salvage work. A Government White Paper set out proposals for the reorganisation of Greater London Council and Metropolitan Counties in the mid-1980s. It was indicated that fire brigades in these areas would be administered by a joint board of district council nominees.

Organisation of the Fire Service

The whole of Britain is covered by public fire brigades offering a free service for extinguishing fires. Following the 1972 Local Government Act, the provision of fire services in the UK became the responsibility of administrative counties in the mid-1970s.

It is the duty of every fire authority in Great Britain to make provision for firefighting purposes and particularly to secure:

a. The services for their area of a fire brigade and such equipment as is necessary to meet efficiently all normal requirements

b. The efficient training of the members of the fire brigade

c. Efficient arrangements for dealing with calls for assistance and for summoning members of the fire brigade

It is the duty of every fire authority in Great Britain to make provision for fire-fighting.

d. Efficient arrangements for obtaining for firefighting purposes information about buildings and property in the area, the availability of and means of access to water supplies, and other material local circumstances
e. Efficient arrangements for preventing or mitigating damage to property resulting from measures taken in dealing with fires
f. Efficient arrangements for giving advice on fire prevention, restriction of the spread of fires and means of escape in case of fire.

The fire authority is also required to take reasonable measures to ensure that an adequate supply of water is available for firefighting.

Each fire authority is required to prepare an establishment scheme for its area and to make arrangements for mutual assistance, generally known as reinforcement schemes, with neighbouring fire authorities. Under such arrangements a fire authority may supplement the services of a neighbouring authority at a large fire, or provide reinforcements at any fire in the area of another authority if it can provide those reinforcements more readily than the authority in whose area the fire has occurred.

The Fire Authority in Northern Ireland is charged with the same duties and responsibilities in respect of firefighting and advising on fire prevention as are the authorities in Great Britain.

Fire authorities have considerable say in the running of their Brigades although central control is exercised by the Home Secretary, Secretary of State for Scotland and the Northern Ireland Department of the Environment. Some examples of powers given to these central bodies include:
1. The establishment of central training institutions and one or more local training centre
2. Provision of pension schemes
3. The appointment of assistant inspectors and certain other officers in the Fire Service Inspectorate
4. In certain instances to require authorities to combine for firefighting purposes.

ADVISORY AND NEGOTIATING PROCEDURES

The Home Secretary and the Secretary of State for Scotland are advised by the appropriate Central Fire Brigades Advisory Council on matters affecting fire brigades as a whole, while conditions of service, ranks and pay are dealt with by the National Joint Council for Local Authorities' Fire Brigades, on which the local authorities and members of the brigades are represented. The National Joint Council for Local Authorities' Fire Brigades is the standing body whose function is the supervision (from a national point of view) of all matters relating to conditions of service of fire personnel by virtue of the Fire Service Acts 1947–1959, other than Chief Fire Officers and Firemasters.

INSPECTORATE

The Fire Services Act 1947 provides for the appointment of Inspectors, Assistant Inspectors and other officers who are required to discover how fire authorities operate and who also offer advice on technical matters.

Fire brigades are inspected annually and Her Majesty's Chief Inspector of Fire Services sends a Report to the Home Office each year on local authority fire brigades in England and Wales.

Her Majesty's Inspectors of Fire Services for Scotland are appointed by Royal warrant and, along with assistant inspectors, they report on fire brigades and advise the Secretary of State on the exercise of his functions under the Fire Services Act, giving guidance and advice to brigades when necessary. Her Majesty's Chief Inspector of Fire Services also acts in that capacity for Northern Ireland.

Inspectors keep abreast of modern fire-fighting techniques and technology; in 1982–83, for instance, one Inspector took twelve months' study leave at the Fire Research Station of the Department of the Environment.

For the purposes of inspection, England and Wales are divided into inspection areas—London Fire Brigade, Western Area, Southern Area, Northern Area and Eastern Area. To take an example, the Southern Area is under the auspices of HM Inspector A. A. Winning, CBE, whose territory takes in seventeen brigades, including Avon, Devon, Somerset, Wiltshire and Kent.

FIRE COVER STANDARDS

Section 1(1) of the Fire Services Act 1947 places a duty on every fire authority to make provision for firefighting purposes, but the precise standards to which this duty must be fulfilled are not specified in legislation.

'Class "A" Risks' include areas with factory, commercial and office property.

The levels to which fire cover is provided are governed to a large extent by standards recommended by the Home Office. The current recommended standards were set out in a Home Office Fire Service Circular 43/1958 (in Scotland, SHHD Circular 9334) which recommended that fire cover provision should be provided in accordance with the risk category of particular areas, as follows.

Class 'A' Risk: applying to larger industrial and commercial cities, and including congested central areas with department stores, factory, commercial and office property and any adjacent congested areas. In 'A' risk areas, the recommended first attendance is two pumps within a maximum of five minutes, and one further pump within eight minutes.

Class 'B' Risk: normally applying to concentrated building areas of large towns not falling within Class 'A', and to any other areas containing a number of dispersed industrial risks. In 'B' risk areas, the recommended first attendance is one pump within a maximum of five minutes, and one further pump within eight minutes.

Class 'C' Risk: normally applying to built-up areas of towns exceeding about 5,000 population, and not falling within Class 'A' or 'B'. The recommended first attendance in 'C' risk areas is one pump within eight to ten minutes.

Class 'D' Risk: including all risks not falling within categories 'A' to 'C', except remote rural areas, and High Risks described below. The recommended first attendance in 'D' risk areas is one pump within twenty minutes.

High Risks: in addition to the four general categories above, the Circulars recommended that extra cover above 'A' risk standards should be provided for certain small areas, such as large docks with associated commercial and warehouse buildings, and highly concentrated commercial and business areas where narrow streets and high buildings create a serious risk of fire spread. It was recommended that such areas should be treated as isolated risks and given a predetermined attendance.

The Green Paper on *Future Fire Policy* (1980) also contains references to the distribution of fire stations, manpower and appliance resources in different risk areas.

OPERATIONAL METHOD AND COMMUNICATION

Each fire authority must appoint a Chief Officer (Firemaster in Scotland) to be the principal administrative and executive figure for the fire services in its area. This appointment is approved in England and Wales by the Home Secretary, in Scotland by the Secretary of State for Scotland, and in Northern Ireland by the Department of the Environment. The Chief Officer or Firemaster is responsible to the fire authority for ensuring that the fire brigade and its administrative HQ are organized and managed in accordance with policy, except that in Northern Ireland these functions are divided between the Chief Fire Officer and the secretary of the authority (the latter being the chief administrative officer).

All brigades have a central headquarters for operational control, and in most brigades local control is exercised by Divisional Commanders in charge of the geographical divisions into which most areas are divided.

The Divisional Commander is generally responsible for the operational efficiency of his division and for dealing with any outbreaks of fire in it, together with the organisation of the fire prevention service. In densely populated or highly industrialised areas of the larger towns, the Divisional Commander has at his disposal a staff of whole-time officers and men; in other parts of the country, such as county divisions with one or two smaller towns surrounded by rural areas, the staff consists of a smaller number of whole-time members supported by retained members of appropriate rank.

COMMUNICATION

Communication arrangements for dealing with fires can be placed in three categories as follows: first, the means by which the public should inform the fire service of the existence of a fire; secondly, the methods used by the service to mobilise its resources; and thirdly, the means by which firemen engaged in firefighting send back reports on the position and call for any additional help required.

The main method of communication by a member of the public is by use of the Telecom telephone network, over which the caller obtains priority by dialling 999. The Telecom operator connects the caller to the fire brigade control centre responsible for alerting and dispatching the nearest fire appliances to the incident.

Another method by which fire calls may be made is by 'fire telephone'. This is a telephone directly connected, by private wire, to the fire brigade control or, in some cases, to commercial central alarm stations. Fire telephones are only installed in premises which are constantly manned, such as hospitals. Another form of fire telephone, known as a 'running call telephone', is usually provided outside fire stations for use by the public when the fire station is unattended.

Warning of fire may also be given by private automatic fire detector systems. In response to fire conditions, sensing devices installed in the protected premises actuate local alarms and automatically transmit an alarm signal either direct to the fire brigade control or to a commercial central alarm station. Commercial central alarm stations are continuously manned and relay fire calls, by direct circuits, to fire brigade control centres.

Fire brigades use special remote control and communications systems for alerting fire station crews and dispatching fire appliances to fires and other incidents. Various alerting systems are used including alarm bells or public address systems on whole-time stations, while at part-time stations the firemen's radio alerter system calls out retained personnel.

Nowadays fire service control and communications arrangements are usually centralised on a brigade basis, the central control rooms being staffed by specialist personnel and equipped to accept emergency calls and dispatch speedily the appropriate appliances and equipment. Predetermined arrangements and a constantly updated record of resource availability ensure that the nearest appliances and equipment, irrespective of administrative boundaries, are sent to incidents.

Special appliances and equipment form part of the predetermined first attendance at special risks.

Some salient areas in communication procedures are epitomised by the inauguration of new mobilising and control systems to replace the outmoded VF System 'A', and new alerters for summoning retained personnel. A replacement programme of mobile radio schemes is well under way, encouraged by the 1979 World Administrative Radio Conference—during 1981, for instance, it was announced that VHF channels for fire service wide area mobile radio-systems would be in the 70/80 MHz band. Furthermore,

a channel bandwidth of 12½ KHz would be utilised, the Home Office supplying systems using Amplitude Modulation. In 1985, the Home Office Directorate of Telecommunications placed a large order to the value of £18 million for over 25,000 vehicle radios for police forces and fire brigades throughout England and Wales.

A recurrent problem of the 1980s has been interference from so-called Citizen Band radio equipment operating from private cars and premises, and, following joint tests by the Directorate of Telecommunications and Kent Fire Brigade during 1982, it was suggested that under normal operating circumstances, transistory low level interference from legal CB equipment could be received from time to time on fire service wavelengths.

An increased number of first line appliances are being equipped with 'walkie-talkie' hand sets allowing messages to be passed over a relatively short distance, which is especially useful at incidents where communication between the fireground and base Pump or Control Unit is essential.

Many fire authorities in Britain have been changed to accommodate computerised procedures like new computerised control systems. Following the amalgamation of fire brigades in the mid-1970s, Strathclyde Fire Brigade decided to commission the RFL Firecat mobilising equipment in 1981, the complete installation becoming fully operational in 1984, a further development being the installation of a microcomputer-based command and control

Predetermined attendance arrangements are operated at major incidents such as this rail crash in East Sussex.

system to integrate the call out systems under one control area. This serves as an instance of a large brigade utilising modern communication and control technology.

FIRE PREVENTION

Fire Prevention plays an important rôle in the fire service and fire authorities are concerned with fire prevention measures required under a variety of statutes, such as the 1936 Public Health Act, Gaming Act of 1968 and the 1971 Fire Precautions Act.

Close liaison is maintained with local building authorities, and, when constructing and designing buildings such as old people's homes, the combined expertise and co-operation of designer, contractor and maintainer are required. The contribution that defective building service installations can make to the rapid spread of smoke and fire has long been recognised, and today the computer provides a useful help in fire prevention and location. From a single point, total management of the environmental conditions within a building can be controlled where a single cable can carry signals giving details on the state of the fire alarm. However, failure of this cable could produce chaos and so fire prevention officers have to check installations very carefully.

Some of the main fire prevention areas in which the fire service is involved are the design of buildings to prevent spread of fire; fire detection and alarm systems; automatic systems for fire suppression; the choice and testing of building materials, and the means of escape from fire and safety of occupants. In association with this, the effectiveness of the 1980 Housing Act has been reviewed recently in an attempt to enforce proper means of escape from fires in hostels, flats and multi-occupied houses, and the mid-1980s are likely to see the publication of a code of guidance on fire safety in such dwellings. The definition of a house of multiple-occupation may be found in the 1969 Housing Act (Section 58) which regards such a building as 'a house which is occupied by persons who do not form a single household'.

Research into the effects of ambient conditions on smoke detection and behaviour of fire detectors is an on-going process at the Fire Research Station of the Department of the Environment; a recent study (1983–84) looks at causes of false alarms from automatic fire detection systems and an examination of life safety applications of sprinkler systems.

Most buildings to which the public resort and in which people are employed are required by law to have safe means of escape from fire and other ancillary precautions, but fire precautions are not, as a rule, required by law in private dwellings, so that education and publicity are the principal means of promoting fire safety in the home. Some fire authorities conduct house-to-house visiting campaigns to advise occupiers on measures to reduce the risk of fire, while national fire prevention campaigns are also held periodically, during which the publicity efforts of the fire authorities are supplemented by advice and assistance from central bodies, including Government departments, and other interested organisations. In addition, the fire service gives lectures and demonstrations on all aspects of fire safety to a wide variety of organisations in both the public and private sectors, including

industrial and commercial firms, hospitals, schools, and clubs and associations of all kind.

The fire service gives lectures on all aspects of fire safety.

Non-governmental bodies concerned with problems of fire prevention include the British Insurance Association and the Fire Protection Association. The British Insurance Association has a general concern over the whole field of insurance. The Fire Protection Association was founded in 1946 by the Fire Offices' Committee as a non-profit-making association, to be the national advisory centre for industry and the general public on the protection of life and property against fire. Through the study of fire problems, fire reports, and collaboration with Government departments and industry, the association has built up an extensive fund of knowledge and experience, which is disseminated through a fire information service from which employers are able to get publicity material about fire prevention and control. The associate members of the association include Government departments, local authorities, fire brigades, and the major industrial and commercial companies in the United Kingdom, together with a considerable representation of overseas interests.

Fire resisting doors and smoke control doors form integral parts of modern buildings and it is interesting to note that standard fire resistance testing began in 1889 when the British Fire Prevention Committee opened Europe's first fire testing station in London, the modern Fire Research Station housed at Borehamwood, Hertfordshire. British Standards tests have been applied to doors over the years; in 1951, for instance, a specification for a one-hour fire check door was added, present methods of test for fire resistance appearing in BS 476 : Part 8 (1972). Currently, there is no standard test method for assessing resistance to smoke penetration of fire doors, but this will form a future part (Part 31) of BS 476 in 1984–85.

Some sources would suggest that fire authorities had little national guidance available to them on the standard of fire precautions relating to places of public entertainment, and the Home Office drew up a national advisory standard which could be used by fire authorities as a reference document in offering advice to licensing authorities.

Towards the close of 1983, various authorities received draft regulations and a guidance document taking into account the 1982 Amendment Regulation concerned with a revision of the Cinematograph (Safety) Regulation of 1955.

All UK Brigades have qualified Fire Prevention Officers, and courses in Fire Prevention are held at the Fire Service Technical College—there were four Fire Prevention Basic Courses in 1982, attended by 84 students, while the six specialist courses catered for 168 students. A further five Fire Prevention Refresher Courses accommodated 124 Fire Prevention Officers.

FINANCE AND INCIDENTS

The cost of local fire services is met by the fire authorities, but they also have an Exchequer contribution, within the rate support grant. The amount of contribution follows discussions between local authorities and Government. In Northern Ireland, the Department of the Environment bears the cost of regional fire services, part of the net expenditure being recouped by a regional rate which helps to pay the cost of local government services provided by the central Government. Total expenditure for recent years, including local authority expenditure and costs borne by the Home Office, is shown below for the fire service in England and Wales.

Financial Year	Expenditure £Million	Amount attributable to employee costs £Million
1980/81	419.83	352.92
1981/82	485.17	417.46
1982/83 (Provisional)	547.94	454.02

Speaking about 1984/5, the Parliamentary Under Secretary of State, Lord Elton, said that the pressure on local authorities to restrain expenditure would continue, but that the current expenditure provision would increase significantly by some £300 million over the existing provision for 1984/85 in the Government's public expenditure plan.

INCIDENTS

The last decade has produced considerable increase in the number of calls attended by the Fire Service. The direct cost of damage to buildings and goods destroyed by fires in Britain in 1975 amounted to an estimated £226 million at a time when annually there were well over 1,000 fires directly causing at least £10,000 worth of damage each.

One of the many property fires
in the mid-1970s.

There are some 94,000 special
service calls a year, many of
which involve road traffic
accidents.

1975 FIRE CALLS ATTENDED

	England and Wales	Scotland	Northern Ireland
Fires (involving property)	121,500	27,296	4,253
Small fires, including grass and heath fires	168,100		4,751
Chimney fires	36,700	4,059	2,160
Sub Total	326,300	31,355	11,164
False Alarms			
Given with good intent	51,000	8,410	1,080
Due to electrical or mechanical fault	18,000		113
Malicious	59,000	4,992	1,056
Sub Total	128,000	13,402	2,249

1975 SPECIAL SERVICES

	England and Wales	Scotland	Northern Ireland
Emergency (including road accidents)	50,400	3,436	195
Others	9,600		157
Sub Total	60,000	3,436	352
Total—all calls	514,300	48,193	13,765

Damage following a fire in an occupied building.

In the mid-1980s, there are some 130,000 fire calls a year involving property received by brigades in England and Wales, the total of special service calls made amounting to about 94,000 a year, a noticeable increase being apparent in humanitarian or emergency incidents other than road accidents, such as spillages of dangerous substances or people trapped in lifts. The mid-1980s brings the total number of fire calls for England and Wales to some 303,000 a year, while the total number of false alarm calls for 1983 was 196,976. Fires in occupied buildings number about 81,000 in England and Wales, 12,000 in Scotland while Northern Ireland has some 2,250 such fires a year, with the majority taking place between 1600 and 2000 hours in England and Wales.

The cost of fires has soared in the 1980s and one need look only at the Amoco Oil Refinery fire in Wales in 1983 to appreciate this rise, the incident in question costing some £10 million. During 1984, one fire at a rail depot in Ayr caused damage estimated at £1.6 million. In July the same year, fire in England, Scotland and Wales cost an estimated £34 million.

MEMBERS OF THE FIRE SERVICE

Britain's fire-fighting personnel is composed of whole-time, retained and volunteer men and women together with fire fighters maintained by the Ministry of Defence, airports and industrial/private brigades. Recent figures show the whole-time establishment of local authority fire brigades

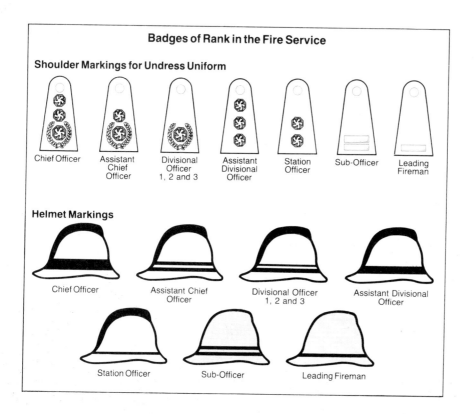

Badges of Rank in the Fire Service

Shoulder Markings for Undress Uniform

Chief Officer | Assistant Chief Officer | Divisional Officer 1, 2 and 3 | Assistant Divisional Officer | Station Officer | Sub-Officer | Leading Fireman

Helmet Markings

Chief Officer | Assistant Chief Officer | Divisional Officer 1, 2 and 3 | Assistant Divisional Officer

Station Officer | Sub-Officer | Leading Fireman

in England and Wales to be 37,169, although the total number of men and women serving in permanent posts is 35,703.

WHOLE-TIME FIRE PERSONNEL

The principal ranks in the fire service are: Chief Officer; Assistant Chief Fire Officer; Deputy Chief Officer; Senior Divisional Officer; Divisional Officer; Assistant Divisional Officer; Station Officer; Leading Fireman; Fireman.

In Scotland, ranks are similar, except that the Chief Fire Officer and Assistant Chief Fire Officer have the titles Firemaster and Assistant Firemaster.

Fire brigades also have non-uniformed staff who work in offices, store-rooms or in brigade workshops.

Those seeking appointments as whole-time members of fire brigades are expected to comply with minimum requirements; men/women should be aged between 18 years and 30 years or up to 34 inclusive for ex-servicemen/women, and must not measure less than 5 ft 6 in (1.68 m) in height. Potential recruits should have a chest measurement of not less than 36 in (91 cms) with a 2 in (5 cms) expansion and should be in good physical shape.

Operational recruits to the fire service are required to undergo a medical examination and physical tests and, although no formal educational qualifications are required, candidates must undergo a series of aptitude tests.

Unlike the Police and Armed Services, a two-tier system of entry does not exist in the fire service, promotion being through the rank structure.

The rank markings of these senior officers are clearly visible as they talk in front of an ERF/Simon SS 85 (1970) Hydraulic Platform.

For promotion to ranks above fireman/woman, candidates take promotion examinations organised by the Fire Service's Central Examinations Board by arrangement with the Local Government Training Board. These examinations require attainment in both practical tests and in written technical examinations.

Appointments to higher ranks are made by selection from ranks not below station officer, following advertising in appropriate publications.

Duty Systems

Shift Fire Station. Usually full-time shift fire stations have watches (Red, White, Blue, Green) each working an eight-day rota of two day shifts, two night shifts and the next four days off duty, spent off the fire station, fire personnel working in two shifts from 0900 to 1800 and from 1800 to 0900.

Day Manning System. This system is employed in areas of lesser risk, the fire station being manned by whole-time members during the day and by the same personnel performing retained duties at night, supplemented where necessary by retained personnel who may provide cover during the day and night, often manning the second pumping appliance.

Day manning fire fighters are in the station from 0900 to 1800, and, like retained men, are on alerter contact outside these hours, their living quarters usually situated close to the fire station.

Examples of appliances at day manning stations can be seen in Staffordshire where Tamworth accommodates a Bedford Water Ladder, Ford Water Tender and an ERF Water Tender Spare Appliance (OBF 197J).

A day manning fire station, Tamworth, Staffordshire. On the left is a Bedford KC/ Carmichael Water Ladder; the Ford 1114 Water Tender has CFE bodywork (1978).

Junior Fire Personnel

Some fire authorities operate junior schemes whereby qualified young people aged 16–17 years are trained to become fully operational members when they reach the age of 18 years. During 1976 30 whole-time juniors were recruited, of whom three left the service and sixteen were promoted to firemen in England and Wales, but in the early 1980s the actual strength in England and Wales was about 20 per year.

RETAINED PERSONNEL

Retained fire personnel usually have other employment in addition to being fire fighters, the retained service being represented by members from divers professions and backgrounds. The establishment for retained firemen is 17,345 although the number of retained personnel is about 15,890 and since some are not available for calls throughout a 24-hour period, the effective unit is some 13,170, representing one-third of Britain's fire fighting force.

Retained members are required to live close to the fire station and in the event of their being required, a pocket alerter emits a bleeping tone, activated by brigade control on receipt of a 999 telephone call. On arrival at their fire station, retained personnel are informed of the job, address and number of appliances required by teleprinter or by direct telephone.

Norfolk retained firemen tackle a blaze, crews coming from Sheringham in a Dodge/CFE Water Ladder (YCL 10S) and Cromer in a Dodge/HCB-Angus Water Ladder (GEX 394N). This retained station also has a Dodge/ERF Water Tender (SAH 458R).

Retained fire stations are manned entirely by retained personnel and are located in rural and semi-rural areas, men often being first in attendance at motorway incidents in open country. Jobs such as house fires and road traffic accidents are dealt with by retained personnel in whose area the incident occurs. Retained stations have one or more Water Ladder/Tender and in some cases four-wheel drive machines, Water Carriers, or Rapid Intervention Vehicles for use at road traffic accidents.

In some areas a fire station may be run almost entirely by retained personnel with one or more whole-time junior officer attached to it, examples of 'nucleus manned' stations being located at such places as Selby (North Yorkshire), Malvern, Ross-on-Wye (Hereford and Worcester) and Acle (Norfolk), this last station housing a Dodge/ERF Water Tender (NVG 891P). Generally speaking, retained fire stations are manned by retained personnel with retained officers in charge.

A retaining fee is paid to all members quarterly, the amount payable being based on the national scale and dependent on the obligations which a member undertakes. A turnout fee is paid if a member leaves the station as part of the crew of an appliance to attend a fire or some other incident. Where a retained member has become entitled to a Turnout Fee or an Attendance Fee and remains on duty on that occasion for more than one hour from the time the fee first became payable, he is entitled to extra payments in respect of each hour's duty after the first hour. An Attendance Fee is payable to a retained member who attends at his station in response to a call within a reasonable time but is not entitled to a Turnout Fee in respect of that attendance. Where a retained member undertakes in addition to his other obligations to perform work in connection with the functions of the brigade, he may be paid at the hourly rate. Bounties are payable on completion of 10, 15, 20, 25, 30 and 35 years qualifying service respectively, at the rate appropriate to the number of years qualifying service and the rank held at the date of qualification.

VOLUNTEERS

There are some 80 volunteer fire fighters in England and Wales with about 1,500 based in Scotland. Equipment is a *mélange* of trailer pumps and vans, the latter often based on Bedford CF vehicles, although the half a dozen volunteer stations in England and Wales have Water Tenders located at places such as Hartland, Kingston (Devon) and Peterborough Volunteer Fire Brigade (Cambridgeshire).

CONTROL ROOM STAFF

Every fire brigade depends on a control room receiving details of emergency calls and in turn calling out the desired appliances from fire stations within the brigade's boundaries.

There are approximately 1,020 women and 490 men working in England and Wales as control room staff, some places having part-time control room staff working next to whole-time colleagues, for example, in Lancashire, Suffolk and Powys. Larger authorities will require more control room staff than the smaller brigades, with South Yorkshire County Fire Service relying on 38 people, Merseyside County Fire Brigade 72, Strathclyde Fire

The Highlands and Islands Fire Brigade owns several Bedford CF vans used by volunteers. Carrying the old name of Northern Fire Brigade, this vehicle operates from Fort Augustus.

Control room staff at Tayside deal with incoming calls.

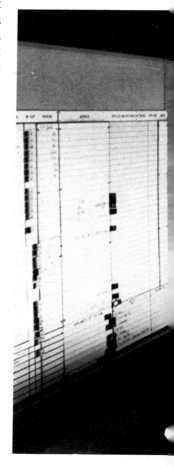

48

49

Brigade 120, West Glamorgan County Fire Service 18 and Tayside Fire
Brigade on 20 control room staff.

There are ranks among control room personnel including Principal Controller, Senior Controller and Control Operator.

FIRE FIGHTING OUTSIDE LOCAL AUTHORITIES

In addition to fire cover provided by local authorities, other fire-fighting
forces take in airport brigades, industrial brigades and those operated by the
Armed Forces.

AIRPORT FIRE BRIGADES

The British Airport's Authority's Chief Fire Officer is responsible for the
organisation and training of the Authority's Fire Service and for fire
prevention at its airports—Stansted, Gatwick, Heathrow, Prestwick,
Edinburgh, Aberdeen and Glasgow, this last airport modernised in
1984–85. The Civil Aviation Authority (CAA) provides fire protection and
organisation at CAA airfields and technical installations in Great Britain and
Northern Ireland, personnel receiving training at the Training School based
at Teesside Airport.

The Dodge/HCB-Angus RIV with Teesside Airport Fire and Rescue Service.

The type of airfield fire/crash tenders depends on local requirements, with the two principal models being Rapid Intervention Vehicles (RIVs) and the larger foam-carrying vehicles. An instance of an RIV is the Chubb model found throughout the world and at Aberdeen, Edinburgh, Gatwick, Glasgow, Heathrow, Prestwick and Stansted airports, and at the Fire Training School; an interesting model with West Sussex Fire Brigade is stationed at Crawley (08), registration JPO 646P, received during 1976. RIVs also come on Range Rover, Reynolds Boughton chassis and Dodge chassis, examples being an RB Apollo/Carmichael, which came into service at Birmingham Airport during 1983, capable of reaching 50 mph in under 20 seconds, or the Dodge/HCB Angus at Teesside Airport. 1984–85 saw a prototype light foam tender demonstrated to the seven BAA airports, the machine being built on a Gloster Saro 4 × 2 chassis with 4 × 4 capability. It is designed to give a low centre of gravity, has a cruising speed of 65–70 mph and a bumper-mounted 300 gallons per minute monitor operated from inside the cab.

In the medium and larger range of aircrash vehicles one could consider the Gloster Saro Javelin, Chubb Protector 2, and a Reynolds Boughton/Angloco aircrash tender recently put into service at Leeds-Bradford Airport. The latter, a 8400 model, has a water-carrying capacity of 1,350 UK gallons and

Leeds Bradford Airport's Reynolds Boughton/Angloco Air Crash Tender.

a foam compound capacity of 150 UK gallons, while the water/foam discharge rate is 900 UK gallons per minute. The self-aspirating monitor projects a jet of foam up to 200 ft while the appliance is moving or stationary. In addition to this machine, Leeds-Bradford Airport possesses a Rescue Tender 1973, Forward Control Land Rover built by Carmichael; a Foam Tender 1976, Unipower, built by Carmichael; a Foam Tender 1966, Bedford 4 × 4 built by Foamite; and a Water Tender 1954, Bedford 4 × 4 Green Goddess. Mid-1984 saw delivery of a Rapid Intervention Vehicle—Reynolds Boughton Apollo 4 × 4/Carmichael.

There are of course numerous private airfields operating a number of interesting fire appliances, the Duxford Airfield, Cambridgeshire, serving as an instance. Duxford Airfield, part of the Imperial War Museum, houses most of the Museum's aircraft collection, many other large exhibits and the Duxford Aviation Society's collection of British civil aircraft. This former Battle of Britain airfield was constructed during World War One and is located eight miles south of Cambridge.

The flying operations at the airfield are controlled by a joint Imperial War Museum/Cambridgeshire County Council panel. During the Museum's open season, between March and November each year, flying facilities are provided for visitors from Wednesday to Sunday each week. The CAA license flying operations each Saturday, Sunday and Bank Holiday for aircraft up to Category 2. Certain air displays require Category 3 or 4, and pleasure flights are provided in all categories.

The DAS Fire Service provides fire and rescue cover for flying categories 1 to 4 for normal cover as well as special operations and air displays. The service comprises a Divisional Officer (CO), Assistant Divisional Officer (DCO), Station Officer (ACO), four Sub Officers, four Leading Firemen

The fire appliances at Duxford airfield.

and nine Firemen. Personnel are certificated by the CAA after successfully completing annual training courses. Regular training on station and operational exercises ensures continuity. It is the only known Part-time Volunteer Airfield Fire Service in the United Kingdom.

APPLIANCES

RAPID INTERVENTION VEHICLE

> one Land Rover series 2a, 4 × 4, registration number NJE 489R
> 272 litres Premixed AFFF expelled by CA cylinder contents
> 25 kg BCF (portable unit)
> 88 kg Monex powder
> Rescue equipment

FOAM TENDER

> one 20 × fixed monitor, two 10 × hand lines
> Thornycroft Nubian Minor/Sun 6 × 6, registration number SXT 107
> 3636 litres water ⎱ Merryweather
> 454 litres Fluoroprotein foam concentrate ⎰ Centrifugal Pump
> 50 kg BCF
> 88 kg Monex powder
> Rescue equipment

WATER TENDER (FOAM)

> two 10 × hand lines
> one Thornycroft Nubian Minor/Sun 6 × 6, registration number VXN 867
> 4318 litres water ⎱ Merryweather
> 227 litres Fluoroprotein foam concentrate ⎰ Centrifugal Pump
> 44 kg Monex powder
> Rescue equipment

WATER TENDER (RESCUE TENDER)

> Reserve appliance
> Bedford RLHZ HCB/Angus 4 × 4, registration number GFL 990D
> 1818 litres water (premixed AFFF when reserve) HCB Dual Pressure Pump
> 25 kg BCF (portable unit)
> 136 litres premixed AFFF
> When used in Rescue Tender rôle, additional equipment carried includes:
> four CABA, two air lifting bags, Blackhawk Hydraulic rescue equipment,
> eight CABA cylinders, reserve foam concentrate, hose, lines, road cones,
> hose ramps, plus miscellaneous gear.

All appliances carry fixed and portable UHF radio-telephone equipment.

This Ford Transit fire vehicle served with Courtauld's Grimsby Division.

Bordon's Bedford/Carmichael fire appliance has both firefighting and rescue gear.

INDUSTRIAL BRIGADES

Industrial premises and some hospitals maintain their own brigades which feature a variety of interesting appliances designed to meet local requirements. Certain industrial brigades have an agreement with local authorities whereby they will turn out to supplement the public brigade. A typical example of the industrial fire brigade is found at James Walker Group Ltd, Woking, whose risks include spirit solvents, and where 30 whole-time and 24 auxiliary firemen are on call providing a 24 hour cover for its main works and four subsidiary companies within a five-mile radius. The major appliances are an LWB Land Rover (WPK 814G), SWB Land Rover (UPL 995M) and a Ford A 0610 series machine (KPD 807P) designed by the Chief Fire Officer. The latter's forward locker houses an Angus AF100 Unit which has been adapted to produce medium expansion foam, while the cab accommodates a driver and four men.

Taking a further instance of an industrial brigade, Courtaulds plc have impressive fire-fighting arrangements, the Grimsby division possessing these appliances housed in three stations, having relied on some interesting machines in the past, including a Ford Transit fire appliance:

FOAM/WATER TENDER

Thornycroft Nubian. Fully self-contained, having a water tank capacity of 700 gallons and a foam tank capacity of 35 gallons plus a supplementary supply of 20 gallons in 5-gallon polythene cans. The pump is a Coventry Climax 500 gallons per minute fitted with a 'round the pump' proportioner.

PUMP WATER TENDER

Bedford. Having a water tank capacity of 400 gallons and carrying 20 gallons of foam in 5-gallon polythene cans. The pump is a Sigmund FN.5.900 gallons per minute at 100 per square inch, plus a 350 gallons per minute Godiva portable pump.

RESCUE TENDER

Land Rover. Fitted with a built-in generator, medium expansion foam equipment, rescue type breathing apparatus and hydraulically powered lifting equipment.

PUMP SUPPORT TENDER

Austin Gipsy. Having a 500 gallons per minute Godiva pump and being used as a personnel-carrier and towing vehicle.

CONTROL UNIT

Bedford. Equipped with special features to be used for major emergencies and in the rôle as breathing apparatus and fire control.

AMBULANCE

Ford. Fitted to local authority standard.

ARMED FORCES

The Air Force Department Fire Service employs some 2,600 personnel who man over 362 fire appliances in 70 United Kingdom-based fire stations. The Navy Department Fire Prevention Service has responsibility for inspections and fire training in all shore establishments in the Navy Department.

From 1946 until 1961, the Army Fire Service was part of the Royal Army Service Corps, but, since 1961, civilians have taken over the fire service. A typical Army Fire Service station may be found in the garrison town of Bordon, Hampshire, offering fire cover not only for the garrisons of Bordon and Longmoor but also for surrounding villages. There are 25 men at Bordon, working a 42-hour week, four-shift system. Their 1982 Bedford KG/Carmichael is equipped with fire-fighting and rescue gear. Similar army stations are found at several places including Bicester, Marchwood, Kineton, Bramley and Donnington.

The Army also has its own fleet of aircrash trucks, such as the Chubb Protector A-TACT model, and on occasions armed forces send machines to public brigade incidents when required. This occurred at the 1983 Milford Haven Refinery fire when a Royal Air Force Strike Command unit's MK 9 airport crash tender provided valuable assistance.

To appreciate RAF fire vehicles, one can look at RAF Scampton whose recent additions include Range Rover/HCB-Angus TACR Mark 2s. There is a Thornycroft Nubian Major/Dennis Mark 9 CrT and a Bedford/Pyrene Mark 8 CrTa.

3

Training of Fire Personnel

The Fire Services Acts place a duty on every fire authority to secure the efficient training of members of its brigade. The Home Secretary and the Secretary of State for Scotland are also empowered under the 1947 Act to establish central and local training institutions for the fire service as a whole.

In England and Wales and Northern Ireland, recruits and junior ranks in the fire service receive practical training in basic firemanship at training centres run either by their own fire authority or by a neighbouring authority; they may also attend refresher courses at these centres. In Scotland, similar training is carried out at a central training school which is the responsibility of the Scottish Home and Health Department.

A progressive scheme of training for leading firemen/firewomen and above and specialised training courses, including fire prevention courses, are provided centrally for personnel from all brigades at the Fire Service Technical College, for which the Secretaries of State are financially responsible. These institutions are administered by their respective commandants, subject to the general direction of the College Board.

Several of the larger brigades in England and Wales and the brigade in Northern Ireland maintain collective training centres, at which practical instruction is given in various aspects of firefighting, drills, first aid, control-room and watch-room procedure and in allied subjects. In addition, lectures and classroom instruction are given in such subjects as the elementary principles of building construction, hydraulics as applied to fire brigade work, electricity, physics, chemistry and fire brigade law and history. Some centres also provide training in motor vehicle driving, in the use of such special appliances and equipment as Turntable Ladders and in other relevant activities.

The basic training period for recruits to the whole-time fire service is twelve weeks, during which time they receive full pay and may receive free board and lodging. Retained members are required to attend their stations for at least two hours weekly for training and other duties and most brigades are able to arrange special weekend or one-week courses for their retained members at a convenient whole-time station or at one of the collective centres.

Training centres are frequently updated and improved, recent examples being East Sussex Fire Brigade's Training Centre at Maresfield which received a Civic Trust Commendation. The new Cleveland County Fire Brigade Complex features two buildings—the fire house and the main training school, the latter containing lecture room, library, mess, kitchen, lounge and bar and a two-storey sports complex. The fire house accommodates a smoke gallery on two floors and facilities for enacting sewer rescues,

Maresfield Training Centre, East Sussex.

while the first floor of the house is split into two external sections, the ceiling and half of the walls being covered in heat-resistant tiles. Among recent advancements in training, a review of Ability Range Tests for recruits is worth noting, introduced during 1980, based on experience and advice from individual brigades. Similarly, the Drill Book Sub Committee of the Joint Training Committee of the Central Fire Brigades Advisory Council, decided to suspend the 'face to face' method of rescue, following criticism from a number of quarters.

The Joint Training Committee of the Central Fire Brigades Advisory Councils reviewed the training syllabus for whole-time recruits to take account of developments in the fire service since the current syllabus was recommended to fire authorities in Fire Service Circular No. 27/1964.

After consulting the Central Fire Brigades Advisory Council for England and Wales, the Secretary of State has approved a revised syllabus and recommends that it should be adopted by fire authorities as the standard syllabus for the training of whole-time recruits, which should be followed as closely as is practicable.

Firemen being trained in the use of main jets. A Wheeled Escape is in background.

The primary aim of the syllabus is to enable a recruit at the end of his training course to take his place alongside experienced firemen in a brigade. Supplementary training to meet local requirements, such as fire boat and hook ladder training, should be provided at brigade level. Training in hook ladders has been excluded from the new syllabus because the majority of firemen no longer use them operationally, but the exclusion of this training from the recruits' syllabus in no way implies disapproval of the use of hook ladders, and it remains open to brigades who have an operational requirement for this equipment to train their own recruits in its use.

A summary of subjects and total time (hours) allocated to the whole time recruit syllabus is shown:

	Technical	Practical
Firemanship	56	98
Fire Prevention	5	—
Fire Protection and Detection	11	1
Water and Pumps	13	37
Hose	4	4
Ladders	3	49
Knots and Lines	2	10
Standard Tests	1	11
Organisation and Allied Subjects	24	3
First Aid	8	10
Organised Fitness Training	—	45
Examinations	9	4
Discretionary Instructional Periods	38	—
Recreation, Kitting Out, etc.	4	—
Totals	178	272

I. *FIREMANSHIP*

1. Practical Firemanship. General instruction in methods of entry into buildings, fire location and spread. Working in smoke. Methods of searching rooms and buildings. Methods of rescue, bridging of staircases. Safety procedures when at work, escape procedures in case of emergency. Ventilation—correct procedures, and dangers. Use and value of hose reel, diffuser and spray nozzles, jets. Cutting away. Method of dealing with gas cylinders. Street electrical distribution boxes, electric sub-stations, electrical and gas main fires, shutting off supplies—meters and fuse boxes. Domestic installation and luminous discharge tubes. Practical firefighting. Extinguishing various types of fire using extinguishers of various types, hand pumps, hose reel equipment, hose, etc.

2. Breathing Apparatus. Indicate circumstances in which BA is used. Basic description of principles of operation. Demonstration by Instructor. Stage 1 BA Control Procedure BA Communications. Hand over to Stage 2.

3. Building Construction. Instruction in the various types of buildings and building materials—construction of walls, roofs, staircases, windows, hearths, flues, doors, floors and general building terms, etc. Personal safety. Simple principles of air conditioning services.

4. Fire Extinguishers. Construction, care and maintenance, classification of and precautions in use. Standard testing. Practical training on all extinguishers in general use on fire situations. Method of re-charging.

5. Fire Hazards. Talks and films on industrial fires, including electrical, chemical and flammable liquid fires. Radiation hazards and radiac instruments. Use of radiation instruments.

6. Foam. Instruction in the principles of foam and its uses, methods of production, and consumption data for the various types of foam producing equipment. Extinction of fires using foam producing equipment. Drills and

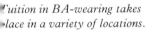

Practical firefighting during training proves invaluable at jobs.

Tuition in BA-wearing takes place in a variety of locations.

practical operation with the various types of foam making branchpipes, generators and inductors in use in the Service.

7. Salvage. Instruction in what salvage means. Description of equipment. Salvage duties during a fire. Reducing water damage, draining, mopping up, reducing smoke damage, etc. Practical use of salvage sheets for covering, draining, mopping up. Use of drying out equipment, etc.

8. Special Services. Definition of special service calls. Description of the methods employed in releasing persons trapped under vehicles, in lifts, sewers, railings, etc. Rescue of animals. Use of jacks and other types of lifting gear, cutting away equipment, etc., for rescue purposes. General approach to road traffic accidents (RTA) and other major accident procedures. Practical use of hydraulic lifting gear and various types of cutting equipment. Rescue from lifts, etc.

9. Small Gear and Equipment. Description of and demonstration with all special tools carried on appliances, including breaking in tools, door openers, cutting away apparatus, hearth sets, rescue gear, hand lamps, floodlights, searchlights, jacks, etc. Talk on equipment carried on ETs and rescue tenders.

Situation Drills: To be introduced when recruits become proficient in handling appliances and equipment. The exercises should be designed to test a recruit's ability to absorb instruction and to use initiative in applying it to practical conditions. Some drills should be arranged during the hours of darkness. The exercises should be progressive and include as many drill manoeuvres as possible.

10. Maintenance of appliances and equipment.

The use of floodlights and searchlights is demonstrated in the three-month training programme. Most Emergency Tenders carry extra lighting facilities and generators.

Recruits are shown equipment carried on Emergency Tenders such as this Ford/CFE based at Shrewsbury, Shropshire.

II. *FIRE PREVENTION*

Introduction to common causes of fires, location of seat of origin, work of Fire Prevention Departments.

III. *FIRE PROTECTION AND DETECTION*

1. **Automatic Fire Alarms.** Instruction in principal types in use; practical demonstration.
2. **Fixed Fire Installations.** For example, rising mains, internal hydrants, foam, BCF.
3. Sprinklers and Drenchers.

IV. *WATER AND PUMPS*

1. **Water as an extinguishing agent.** Pressure and head flow, etc.
2. **Hydrants and Water Supplies.** Types of hydrants; cleaning and testing.
3. **Collector Pumping and Water Relaying.** Positioning of pumps, water tender shuttle service.
4. **Pump and Primers.** Types in use; practical Drills.

V. *HOSE*

1. Construction, care, and maintenance of all types of delivery and suction hose in use.

2. Hose Fittings. Couplings, adaptors, branch pipe nozzles (including fog nozzles and applicators). Branch holders, breechings, collecting heads, strainers, standpipes, hose bandages, hose ramps, etc.

VI. *LADDERS*

1. Ladders, Escape, Extension ladders including 45 ft ladders and carrying down. Use of TLs and HPs. Introductory talk on each type prior to initial practical drill. Escape and Extension ladder drills as per Drill Book, including slipping, pitching, extending, lowering, bridging, line rescues. Use of Everest device. Jets and hose reels working from ladders and Escapes through pump.

Use of TLs and HPs. Picking-up Drill. Practical training in picking up, lowering and carrying an insensible person. (Recruits must be proficient in this drill before being allowed to carry down.)

Training session with a Hydraulic Platform.

Fire personnel learning how to lower an insensible person.

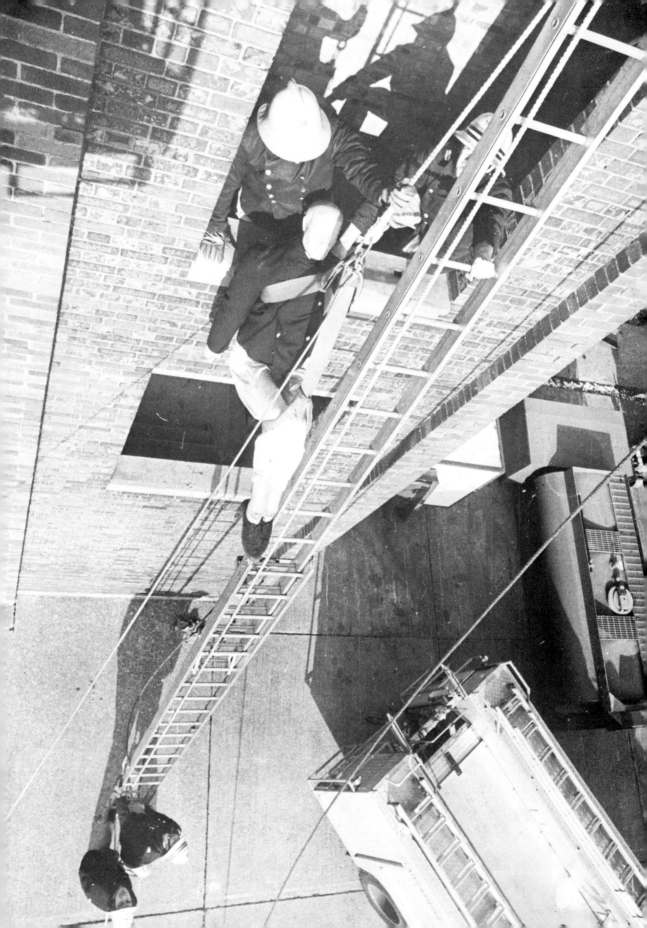

VII. *KNOTS AND LINES*

Types of line; use of individual knots, etc.

VIII. *STANDARD TESTS*

Reasons, types, methods.

IX. *ORGANISATION AND ALLIED SUBJECTS*

1. Talk by Commandant or other Senior Officer, followed by:

2. Talk by a Chief Fire Officer, covering areas of Fire Service life.

3. Final Talk by Commandant.

4. Post entry career prospects.

5. Organisation of the Fire Service, e.g. responsibility of Fire Authorities; rôle of various unions and fire associations.

6. Discipline Code.

7. Communication.

8. Standard messages—'stop', 'informative', etc.

9. Elementary Mobilising Course.

10. Emergency Fire Service Planning.

11. Co-operation with Police and Ambulance Services at incidents.

X. *FIRST AID.*

Theoretical and Practical training in the handling of casualties.

A 'Maxaman' portable resuscitator employed by Cambridge Fire and Rescue personnel during training. The Stonefield P5000 6 × 4 Rescue Tender is based at Cambridge.

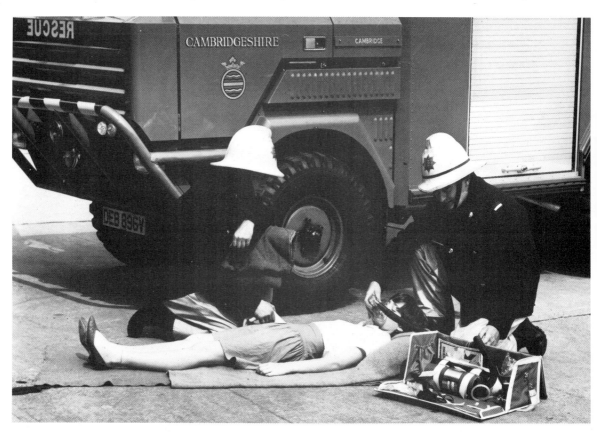

XI. *PHYSICAL EDUCATION.*

Squad drill; organised fitness training; swimming.

XII. *EXAMINATION.*

1. One written and one oral examination each covering technical aspects. Note: On Technical subjects students to obtain a minimum 50 per cent in both oral and written, with an *overall* standard of 60 per cent.
2. Revision and Tests; Practical Examination. Each recruit to be tested in ladder drill, carrying down, escape drill, pump drills, pump operation, knots and lines, and in the use of small gear. Note: Students to obtain a pass standard of 70 per cent.

XIII. *DISCRETIONARY INSTRUCTIONAL PERIODS*

To be used at the discretion of the Commandant, but to include half-hour quiz periods on the subjects taught. (Average of just over three per week.)

XIV. *RECEPTION, KITTING OUT, ALLOCATION OF ACCOMMODATION, ETC.*

Training of fire personnel is an on-going process with operational fire fighters receiving regular drill routines which cover a variety of areas such as rescue, communications and fire appliances. To illustrate this, one can look at the drills offered by Tayside Fire Brigade, the section/phase layout providing a summary of principal areas.

TAYSIDE FIRE BRIGADE
SECTION/PHASE LAYOUT

Section		Phases
A	Fire Prevention 1	Turntable Ladder 1
	Emergency Tender 1	Breathing Apparatus 1
	Special Fires 1	Hydraulic Platform 1
	Fire Service Examinations	Communications
B	Fire Prevention 2	Pump 1
	Practical Firemanship 1	Emergency Tender 2
	Special Fires 2	Breathing Apparatus 2
	Fire Service Examinations	Communications
C	Emergency Tender 3	Pumps 2
	Foam Tender 1	Turntable Ladder 2
	Practical Firemanship 2	Ship Fires 1
	Fire Service Examinations	Communications
D	Fire Service Legislation 1	Pumps 3
	Breathing Apparatus 3	Special Fires 3
	Ship Fires 2	Foam Tenders 2
	Fire Service Examinations	Communications
E	Fire Prevention 3	Breathing Apparatus 4
	Hydraulic Platform 2	Special Fires 4
	Foam Tender 3	Fire Service Legislation 2
	Fire Service Examinations	Communications
F	Pump 4	Fire Prevention 4
	Emergency Tender 4	Special Fires 5
	Foam Tenders 4	Special Fires 6
	Fire Service Examinations	Communications

The phases deal with a variety of topics and some areas are dealt with in four parts. By selecting some of these phases, one can appreciate the detail covered in Drill Routines.

The Tayside Brigade provides a Phase Guide giving further details of areas to be covered. Some topics like Fire Prevention and Emergency Tenders have four phases, whilst Hydraulic Platform drills have two phases.

TAYSIDE FIRE BRIGADE
PHASE GUIDE

Phase 1—Fire Prevention, Part 1

a. Inspecting Premises—Legislation covering the relevant sections of OSRA, Factories Act, Fire Precautions Act, Safety at Work Act, Licensing, Child Minders.
b. Methods of Inspection. Report Writing, Recording of Inspections.
c. Practical Means of Escape, Alarms and Appliances, Automatic Detection.
d. Quiz.

Phase 2—Fire Prevention, Part 2

a. Survey Procedures, Codes of Practice, Plan Drawing, Exercises using Overhead Projectors, Pet Animals Act, Music, Singing and Dancing Act, Caravan Site Legislation and Sprinkler Systems.

Phase 6—Emergency Tender, Part 2

a. Rescue Equipment—Detailed descriptions of the function and purpose of various tools including Cengar Saw, Air Tools, Porto Power, Partner Saw, Electric Tools, Air Bags and Emergency Lighting.
b. Application in Practical Situations.
c. Utilising of ET as main BA Control, BA Control Procedures, Stage I, II and Main Control.

Pump drills and use of hose reel with a Dodge Commando Go8/Carmichael.

Phase 9—Breathing Apparatus, Part 1

a. CABA Airmaster—Description, Function and Operation.

b. Principle of Maintenance and Fault Finding.

c. Stage I, Stage II and Main Control Procedures.

d. BA Exercise, Full Firefighting Gear, Heat and Smoke.

e. Quiz. Lectures on General, Monthly and Annual Checks, Introduction to Test Rig Procedure.

Phase 13—Pumps, Part 1

a. Four and five man pump drills incorporating open water and pressure fed supplies, use of hose reel, and water tender ladder drills. Water Chemistry and Basic Hydraulics (preferably using films or slides covering the subject).

b. Principles of Pumps and Primers as they relate to the stations' working appliances, for example, Dodge, Featherweight pumps.

c. Practical evolutions of pumping techniques with full participation of crews.

d. Quiz.

Phase 17—Turntable Ladder, Part 1

a. Lectures by means of film slides and overhead projector covering the appliances used for Rescue Purposes; Station's Topography of hard standings; siting in relation to buildings and other appliances; use as a staircase and as a crane for sewer rescues.

b. Evolutions in yard dealing with means of overcoming practical difficulties in siting.

c. Exercises at outside locations involving rescues, external staircase and other appliances.

d. Quiz.

Phase 19—Hydraulic Platform, Part 1

a. Vehicles used as a rescue appliance; siting in relation to buildings and other appliances; topography of hard standing in station's area; use of the appliance as a crane.

b. Drills involving techniques described in (a) with participation of crews.

c. Joint exercises involving Hydraulic Platform, with other stations.

d. Quiz.

Phase 20—Hydraulic Platform, Part 2

a. Lectures and drills on the vehicles used as a firefighting platform working with the Emergency Tender and Foam Tender. Drills involving Turbex and P500 Hi-Expansion Foam Generator.

b. Joint drills demonstrating the above techniques.

c. Drills at outside locations on cambers and inclines. Drills and Lectures involving L16A as Water Monitor and Foam Monitor.

d. Drills exclusively for Hydraulic Platform Operators devising techniques to improve their handling capabilities.

Phase 22—Foam Tender, Part 2

a. Lectures on the use of Medium Expansion and Low Expansion Foam

A Ford/CFE Hydraulic Platform used in a drill at Surrey Fire Brigade's Training Centre.

including techniques of application. The foam's sheer strength and stability including one case study of the use of medium expansion foam.

b. Drills incorporating Z2, Z4 and Junior 800, 10X, 5X and variable Foam Inductor.

c. Combined exercise.

d. Quiz.

Phase 25 Practical Firemanship, Part 1

a. Method of entry with reference to Fire Service Act Section 30 and various tools employed.

b. Chimney Fire and Hearth Fires. Drills involving ropework. First Aid and Casualty Handling. Tactical Exercises.

c. Roof fire and Basement fires.

d. High Rise Flats and Quiz.

Phase 27—Ship Firefighting, Part 1

a. Lectures on Fire in Holds and Accommodation Spaces. Fire Spread. Conduction. Convection. Ventilation. Stability.

b. Lecture on Extinguishing Media—CO_2, Hi-Expansion, Medium Expansion, Low Expansion Foam and Water.

c. Exercises using B.A. in the Training Blocks, rigged as ships' accommodation space.

d. Ships' inbuilt fire protection—Communication and Man Power Problems, CO_2 plant continuous discharge and total flooding systems—Topography of Dock Areas.

Special incidents include rescues from aircraft. Lincolnshire Fire Brigade makes use of a 'mock' fuselage for drill purposes.

Phase 29—Special Fires, Part 1, Compressed Gas Cylinders

a. Station Risks, Topography and Store Sites.

b. Firefighting procedures when dealing with Compressed Gas Cylinders including LPG, acetylene, hydrogen, nitrogen, oxygen; their chemistry and physical properties. Fire Prevention measures including correct storage.

c. Exercise in drill yard and at outside locations involving incidents with Compressed Gas Cylinders, construction of dam and subsequent disposal of affected cylinders.

d. Quiz.

Phase 33—Special Fires, Part 5, Refrigeration

a. Scientific principles of Refrigeration including a view of the various refrigerators used locally.

b. Topography of risks on station ground.

c. Visitation to risks, in liaison with Fire Prevention Department.

d. Exercise simulating large refrigerant leak involving BA, Air Lines and Emergency Tender.

e. Case Study into large refrigerant leak.

Phase 36—Fire Service Legislation, Part 2

a. Discipline Code—Employment Protection Consolidation Act.

b. Fire Service Act—Health and Safety at Work Act.

c. Brigade Orders—Brigade Sports and Welfare Association.

d. Routine Orders—Appointments and Promotion Regulations.

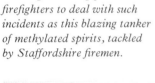

Thorough training permits firefighters to deal with such incidents as this blazing tanker of methylated spirits, tackled by Staffordshire firemen.

Phase 39—Communications, Part 1

a. Brigade Radio Scheme; sites and channels; Radio Procedure; Field Telephone.

b. Visit to Control Room. Lecture on Mobilising Procedure. Introduction to Dictalog Direct Lines. Mascot 70 and stand-by. Card retrieval systems and Emergency Information (Blue Folder).

c. V.F. System A. UHF Radio (Pocket Phone 70) Drills and Lectures. Lectures on the use of exchange telephone (Distress Calls, etc.). Multitone Pocket Alerter System.

d. Mobile Control Unit. Drills and Lectures involving BA with Pocket Phone 70 attachments. Control at incidents. Major Disaster Plan. Exercises using VHF, UHF, Radio and Field Telephone communications.

BA Control Point at a major incident. The machine on the left is a 1971 ERF/HCB-Angus Emergency Tender (TDK 999K).

BREATHING APPARATUS TRAINING

The current trend is to provide a BA set for each man riding a fire appliance and facilities for training at the Fire Service College and at brigade training schools are first class. BA training is carried out during drill periods at retained and whole-time stations using simulated rescue situations.

During 1983–84, a number of improvements have been observed in breathing apparatus training for fire personnel, and a BA-orientation facility was put into operation at Shropshire Fire Service's Shrewsbury Fire Station, one of the first of its kind in the country. The training is surveyed by means of an infrared camera, and facilities exist to video record training sessions as an aid to de-briefing sessions following an exercise.

The new BA training complex at Gloucestershire Fire and Rescue Service has three main areas to provide for teaching, wearing and support, the

Whole-time firemen receive a 58½ hour course on the use of compressed air breathing apparatus.

Picking his way through débris from a factory blaze, this man proceeds to BA Control.

teaching areas having seating for nine students working at individual work benches. There is a total of 63 metres of crawl galleries in the wearing area, while the support areas house a generator room, smoke generator, showers and storeroom.

Fire Service Circular No. 8/1981, *Training of Firemen in Breathing Apparatus*, states that, in order to maintain the distinction between the BA wearer and BA operator, a fireman must not be considered to be qualified or nominated as a compressed air BA-operator until he has completed six months' service on an operational fire station following his basic course in BA. The circular continues that the six-month bar should be lifted, allowing a whole time fireman, who has satisfactorily completed the basic training course in BA following recruit's training course, to be nominated as a BA operator.

Whole-time firemen follow a 58½ hour course on compressed air BA, the syllabus being based on nine eight-hour working days, allowing two fifteen-minute breaks and a one-hour lunch break, providing a total of 58½ hours' instruction time.

Once a BA operator, a fireman has to receive regular training, Staffordshire Fire Brigade, for instance, requiring the following topics to be performed by each individual to at least the minimum frequencies indicated by the training record.

Topic Number	Subject	Content
1	Breathing Apparatus	Breathing Apparatus wearing whilst participating in drills, e.g., hose reel to work, hazchem exercise, the wearing of chemical protection suit, etc. Entrapped procedure should be practised at intervals of not less than three months. Instruction on servicing B.A. sets and ancillary equipment.
2	Breathing Apparatus (Endurance)	Breathing Apparatus wearing in smoke and involving hard work. (Where smoke is not available it should be simulated by working in darkness or dimming out face pieces.)
3	Breathing Apparatus (Guidelines)	Breathing Apparatus wearing involving the use of guidelines.
4	Breathing Apparatus (Communications)	Breathing Apparatus wearing involving the use of communications equipment.
5	Breathing Apparatus (Control Procedures)	Participation in all breathing apparatus control procedures, i.e., Stages I and II and Main Control. Emergency and entrapped procedure (including evacuation procedure).

The contents of a standard cylinder is about 1200 litres while ultra-light cylinders have 2250 litres, and the required safety margin for a compressed air breathing apparatus set is ten minutes. Obviously, the working duration of a BA depends on the work involved, but the assumed average rate of consumption for a compressed air set is 40 litres a minute.

FIRE SERVICE TECHNICAL COLLEGE

The Fire Service Technical College at Moreton in Marsh, Gloucestershire, is known in firefighting circles throughout the world. Some 10,000 visitors

attend courses each year, coming from the United Kingdom and areas such as the USA, Japan, Saudi Arabia and India.

The College offers sophisticated training facilities including a control tower from which the safety of students under training is monitored by recording and measuring temperature, oxygen content, smoke density and carbon dioxide in fireground buildings. These comprise a drill tower of eight floors and a basement containing a smoke and heat generating room; sewers; lift gear; and an industrial block of two floors accommodating a fish and chip shop and warehouse. There is also a three-bedroomed house, breathing apparatus training block plus a simulated ship standing in four

General view of training buildings at the Fire Service Technical College.

feet of water alongside a quay and cargo store: all prerequisities for training the modern fire fighter. Students can also fight fires in a 2,500-gallon oil tanker, two propane gas cylinders and an oil tank. There are some 30 fire appliances at Moreton, which also provides modern dormitories and sports facilities.

A recent development from the Fire Service Technical College (1983) was an improved jet/spray branch developed by the Fire Experimental Unit.

Senior officers take part in an exercise on Moreton's simulated ship.

Delivering 20 to 30 per cent more water than former designs, the new branch was the result of work following on from some 1,000 experiments, which indicated that suitable spray patterns can be achieved by discharging water through a concentric annular orifice formed between an inner core and a moveable outer collar.

Courses offered at the Moreton-in-Marsh College deal with most aspects of the Fire Service, as typified by those available for the 1984–85 period. Junior Officers (Leading Firemen and Sub Officers) have two courses of six weeks' and twelve weeks' duration, providing tuition in fire prevention, operations at fires and fire command leadership. There are three different Fire Prevention courses during 1984–85, the Specialist one lasting a total of fourteen weeks, and Instructors' Courses offering guidance for those employed to teach Breathing Apparatus use.

Retained Junior Officers can attend Moreton's College for one-week courses, incorporating such areas as use of road traffic accident gear, management and breathing apparatus, while Control Room Staff are also accommodated on three-week sessions.

The Fire Service College provides further programmes in such areas as Brigade Command, Fire Investigation Courses and Seminars for Chief Fire Officers and their Deputies. An instance of one course would be that of Brigade Command:-

BRIGADE COMMAND (6 January—22 March 1985)

1. Duration: eleven weeks, including two weeks normally spent away from the College to be used by the student to undertake research and preparation for individual projects.

2. Entry Qualifications: Selection for the course is by the extended interview procedure which officers from Divisional Officer to Assistant Chief Fire Officer may try provided they have attended a Divisional Command Course or its earlier equivalent.

3. The aims of the course are:

a. to train officers in brigade command by enabling them to acquire a knowledge at an advanced level of personnel management both in command on the fireground and in brigade administration.

b. To acquire administrative ability at an advanced level both within the fire service and especially within the context of the government at Chief Officers and member level together with a knowledge of central government.

c. To obtain knowledge of how to promote commission control and profit from research and development in the technical and administrative aspects of fire service work.

d. To develop an appreciation of society and the environment within which the fire service operates both at home and in the European Economic Community.

Fire Fighting Vehicles

Fire authorities in the United Kingdom are required to provide equipment and vehicles under the Establishment Schemes, and a uniform set of equipment such as hoses and couplings allows for interchanging of gear when more than one brigade attends a major incident.

There are certain specifications to be met by the Joint Committee on Design and Development of Appliance and Equipment (JCDD); this is a joint committee of the Central Fire Brigades' Advisory Council (England and Wales) and the Scottish Central Fire Brigades' Advisory Council. Examples of JCDD influence can be seen in a number of areas—the specifications JCDD/3/1, JCDD/4 and JCDD/18 required that exhaust systems should be located away from any combustible material and that the exhaust should be designed in such a way that loose straw or grass could not become lodged in it.

Again, in the early 1980s amendments on ladder stowage referred to the security of the ladder, stating that the mounted height of the lowest point on the ladder normally carried must not be more than 6 ft 6 in (1.98 m) above ground level.

The more common fire appliances in the United Kingdom comprise a chassis supplied by one firm with bodywork coming from another company specialising in this, but sometimes one finds both chassis and body supplied by one Group. A vehicle described as Bedford/Saxon would feature Bedford

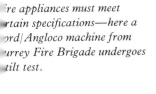

Fire appliances must meet certain specifications—here a Ford/Angloco machine from Surrey Fire Brigade undergoes tilt test.

chassis and Saxon coachwork; other combinations might be ERF/HCB-Angus or Shelvoke and Drewry/Carmichael.

Fire brigades possess a variety of fire vehicles, the more common Water Tender or Water Ladder is the first appliance sent to most jobs, while specialist machines, including Turntable Ladders or Emergency Tenders, may follow should an incident require their attendance. Certain high risk categories necessitate both the specialist machines and Water Ladder vehicles.

WATER TENDERS

These appliances are found frequently in semi-rural districts, although many brigades now provide Water Ladders for these areas. The Water Tender usually has 400 gallons (1818 litres) of water, portable pump, built-in pump together with lengths of hose, breathing apparatus sets and a 30 ft or 35 ft extension ladder. One finds Water Tenders up and down the country as shown below:-

Brigade	Chassis	Body	Registration	Comments
Avon	ERF	HCB-Angus	RHT 999G	1968
	Dodge	HCB-Angus	HAE 881X	1981
Cleveland	Dennis RS	Dennis	EPY 191V	1979, Redcar
Cornwall	Bedford TK	HCB-Angus	SLG 770Y	St Keverne
Gloucestershire	Dodge G1313	Carmichael	BDG 40Y	Cheltenham
Gwynedd	Bedford	HCB-Angus	LJC 31K	Nefyn
Hampshire	Bedford TK	HCB-Angus	A32 OPX	Sutton Scotney
Lancashire	Ford D1114	HCB-Angus	STJ 906M	Bolton le Sands
	ERF		JFV 742N	Tarleton
Somerset	Bedford KG	Saxon SVB	A618 OYA	Taunton
Staffordshire	Ford 1114	HCB-Angus	MFA 473P	Kinver

There have been several cases of disposals of older Water Tenders in recent times, Hertfordshire Fire Brigade acquiring four new Dennis SS Water Ladders which released a number of Water Tenders such as Bovingdon's Bedford/HCB Angus machine (PJH 560D) and Bushey's Dennis F44 (FAR 565G). Royal Berkshire Fire Brigade sold their 1971 Dennis F108 'B' type Water Tender and a 1967 Karrier WB 'B' type during 1984, while Cambridgeshire Fire and Rescue Service offered a number of appliances for sale in 1984–85, including four Bedford Water Tenders: NCE 518H (1970); HEW 148E (1967); AJE 350B (1964); FEW 883D (1966).

During 1985 Somerset Fire Brigade acquired three type 'B' Water Tenders on Bedford KG chassis, built in accordance with Home Office JCDD/3/1 specification.

WATER LADDERS

Water Ladders (WrLs) usually come with a 45-ft (13.5 m) extension ladder, and are becoming increasingly popular with brigades. In addition to carrying a water tank whose normal capacity is 400 gallons (1818 litres), these

appliances accommodate a variety of fire-fighting and rescue gear in lockers and to appreciate the varied equipment carried one can examine a popular marque, the Dennis RS 133. Devon Fire Brigade operates several of these Water Ladders, with a height of 9 ft 11 in, a length of 25 ft 2 in and a width of 7 ft 6 in. Equipment stowed on various parts of the machine is detailed in the accompanying table.

Nearside Front Upper Locker

Floodlamps	2
Blue Flashing Lamp	1
Box Lamp	1
Blue Lens Cover	1
Amber Lens Cover	1
Junction Box	1
Battery Charger	1
Wrecking Bars	2
Bolt Croppers	1
Engineers' Tool Roll	1
Handsaw	1
Aircraft Axe	1
Shovel	1
Pickaxe and Handle	1
Large Axe	1
Sledge Hammer	1
Tripods	2

Nearside Front Lower Locker

FB5X Foam Branch	1
Foam Compound, 5 gallons	4
Pick-up Tube	1
Wooden Blocks in Box	12
Tirfor Winch	1
Tirfor Cable	1
Tirfor Handle	1
Tirfor Straps, 6 ft, 16 ft 4 in (2 m, 5 m)	2
Hydraulic Rescue Set 1	1
Hydraulic Rescue Set 2	1
Eye Bolts	2

Nearside Centre Locker

Hose, $2\frac{3}{4}$ in (70 mm)	6
Hose, $1\frac{3}{4}$ in (45 mm)	1
Hose Short Length, $2\frac{3}{4}$ in (70 mm)	1
Hose Ramps	2
False Spindle	1
Hose Bandages	4
Hose Sling	1
Branch	1
Standpipe (single outlet)	1
'T' Key and Bar	1
Hydrant Cover Key	1
Dividing Breeching	1

Nearside Rear Lower Locker

Hosereel, 60 ft (18 m)	3
Hosereel Branch	1
Winding Handle	1
Wheel Chock	1

Nearside Rear Upper Locker

Chimney Rods	12
Chimney Hose, Rose and Valve Assembly in Wooden Box	1
Bucket, Metal	1
Chimney Mirror in Case	1
Chimney Sheet	1
Chimney Scraper	1
Hand Brush	1
Hand Shovel	1
Floor Cloths	2
Stirrup Pump	1
Hearth Kit Tool Roll	1
Hosereel Adaptor	1
Firemen's Axes	2

Offside Front Upper Locker

Chance Stretcher	1
Hydraulic Cutter and Pump in Box	1
Air Tools in Box:	
Cengar Saw	1
Blades, 6 in	6
Blades, 12 in	3
Spare Spring	1
Zip Gun	1
Chisels, Panel Cutting	2
Chisel, Rivet Cutting	1
Can Green Oil	1
Air Hoses:	
50 ft (15 m) of $\frac{1}{2}$ in (12.5 mm)	2
25 ft (7.5 m) of $\frac{3}{8}$ in (9.37)mm	2
15 ft (4.5 m) of $\frac{1}{4}$ in (6.25mm)	3
BA Cylinder	1
Air Reducing Valve	1
Goggles in Box (pairs)	6

Dust Masks (in Goggles' Box)	6
Rubber Gloves in Box (pair)	1
Blankets	2

Offside Front Lower Locker

Portable Pump	1
Battery Charger	1
Floodlight for LPP	1
Pole for LPP Floodlight	1
Dry Power Extinguisher (20 lbs)	2
Petrol Container, 2-gallon	1
Suction Adaptor, 4 in (100 mm)	1
Oil Can, 1 quart	1
Collecting Head	1
Blank Cap	1

Offside Centre Locker

Hose, $2\frac{3}{4}$ in (70 mm)	7
Hose, $1\frac{3}{4}$ in (45 mm)	1
Branch	1
Hose Sling	1
False Spindle	1
'T' Key and Bar	1
Standpipe (single outlet)	1
Hydrant Cover Key	1
Hose Ramps	2
Hosereel Adaptor	1

Offside Rear Lower Locker

Hosereel, 60 ft (18 m)	3
Hosereel Branch	1
Winding Handle	1
Wheel Chock	1

Offside Rear Upper Locker

Line, 50 ft (15 m), c/w Orange Bag	1
Line, 100 ft (30 m), c/w Green Bag	1
Lowering Line c/o Yellow Bag	1
Guy Line c/w Yellow Bag	1
Salvage Sheets	2

Disposable Salvage Sheets	2
Industrial Gloves (*pairs*)	6
Heat Resistant Gloves (*pair*)	1
Chemical Protection Suits	4
Chemical Protection Gloves (*pairs*)	8
Floor Cloths	4
Bags for Chemical Protection Suits	4

Rear of Appliance

Suction Hose, 4 in (100 mm)	4
Suction Strainer, 4 in (100 mm)	1
Suction Wrenches	2
Hose, $2\frac{3}{4}$ in (70 mm), Flaked	2
Hose, $1\frac{3}{4}$ in (45 mm), Flaked	3
Branch	1
Collecting Head	1
Hay Fork, Four-Prong	4
Ceiling Hook	1
Carriage Key	1

Top of Appliance

Ladder, 13.5 m	1
Ladder, 10.5 m	1
Roof Ladder	1
Short Extension Ladder	1
Beaters	6
Drag Fork	1
Ground Monitor	1

Crew Cab

Folders for 1 (i)(d) & SSC Forms	2
Nominal Roll Board	1
Hazardous Loads' Book	1
Handlamps	6
Minuteman (complete)	1
Harness Knife	1
Whistle	1
Magnescope	1
Reflective Jackets	6
BA Control Board & Watch	1
BA Chinagraph Pencils	2
BA Sets (complete)	4
BA Lamps	4

BA Guideline in Pouch	1
BA Armband	1
BA Tallies (*set*)	1
BA Mask Bags	4
Duster	1
Spare BA Cylinders	3
Fire Station Key	1
Railway Warning Horns	2
First Aid Box	1
Police Slow Signs	2
Vehicle Jack	1
Jack Handle	1
Wheelbrace and Bar	1
Traffic Tape	1
Maps in Map Case (PVC)	1
Map Case (Metal)	1
Message Pad and Pencil	1

Hydraulic Rescue Set 1

Pump and Handle	1
Ram (8-ton)	1
Tube Extension 5 in (127 mm)	1
Tube Extension 20 in (508 mm)	1
Tube Extension 30 in (762 mm)	1
Colour Code Chart	1
Ram Head for 6-ton Ram	1
Serrated Saddle	1
Tube Extension 3 in (76 mm)	1
Tube Extension 10 in (254 mm)	1
Ram (6-ton)	1
Serrated Head for 6-ton Ram	1
Tube Connector Female	4
Slip Lock 10 in (254 mm)	1
Tube Connector Male	1

Hydraulic Rescue Set 2

Baseplate, flat	1
Vee Bases, 90°	2
Wedge Head	1
Dome Rubber, 5 in (127 mm)	1
Dome Rubber, $3\frac{1}{4}$ in (83 mm)	1
Tape Measure, 10 ft (3 m)	1
Wedgie	1
Alligator Jaw Spreader	1
Spreader Ram Toe, small	1

Spreader Ram Toe, large	1

Hearth Kit

Bolster Chisel	1
Chisel, 8 in (203 mm)	1
Chisel, 12 in (305 mm)	1
Wood Chisel	1
Lump Hammer	1
Claw Hammer	1
Floorboard Saw	1
Jemmy	1
Wire Cutters	1
Nail Punch	1
Adjustable Spanner, 10 in (254 mm)	1

Engineers' Tool Kit

Adjustable Spanner, 6 in (152 mm)	1
Adjustable Spanner, 10 in (254 mm)	1
Hacksaw	1
Hacksaw Blades	3
Spade Screwdriver small	1
Spade Screwdriver medium	1
Spade Screwdriver large	1
Phillips Screwdriver small	1
Phillips Screwdriver medium	1
Phillips Screwdriver large	1
Open Ended Spanner, 14–15 mm	1
Open Ended Spanner, 12–13 mm	1
Open Ended Spanner, $\frac{3}{8}$ in—$\frac{5}{16}$ in W	1
Open Ended Spanner, $\frac{7}{16}$—$\frac{3}{8}$ in W	1
Ring Spanner, $\frac{1}{4}$ in—$\frac{5}{16}$ in W	1
Ring Spanner, $\frac{7}{16}$ in—$\frac{1}{2}$ in W	1
Ring Spanner, $\frac{1}{2}$ in—$\frac{7}{16}$ in AF	1
Ring Spanner, $\frac{9}{16}$ in—$\frac{5}{8}$ in AF	1
Pliers	1
'C' Spanners	2
Stilson, 10 in (254 mm)	1
Lift Keys (where appropriate)	1
Blank Cap for LPG Cylinder	1
Meter Box Key	1

The nearside locker contents of a Dennis RS with Devon Fire Brigade (CTT 288Y) on the run at Plymouth.

The offside lockers on CTT 288Y.

The Dodge/Carmichael machine is based at Dolgellau, Gwynedd, where a Land Rover/Carmichael Rescue Pump is also on the run (OJC 285S).

Typical combinations of Water Ladder marques would be Dodge/Carmichael, Bedford/HCB-Angus and Ford/HCB-Angus, all brigades relying heavily on Water Ladders as first-line appliances. Greater Manchester County Fire Service, for instance, operates some one hundred such machines (including reserves), East Sussex Fire Brigade owns two dozen, West Yorkshire Fire Service about 55 while Merseyside County Fire Brigade's Water Ladders number approximately 40. Examples of recent acquisitions are:

Brigade	Model	Registration	Comments
Avon	Dodge G1313/ Merryweather	NEU 560/3Y	Southmead, Brisling- ton, Kingswood, Weston Super Mare
Central Region	Dodge G1313/ Fulton & Wylie	WMS 254Y	Alloa
Cleveland	Dennis SS133/ Dennis	A988 FAJ	Billingham
Greater Manchester	Dennis RS131/ Dennis	A22/32 JDB	To seven fire stations
Gwynedd	Dodge/Carmichael	GCC 334Y	Dolgellau
Hertfordshire	Dennis SS133	A317/20 NRO	Cheshunt, Stevenage, Hemel Hempstead, Garston
Lincolnshire	Bedford TK/HCB- Angus	A701 PVL	Boston
Northampton- shire	Bedford KG/Saxon	A99 UBD	Moulton
Somerset	Bedford KG/Saxon	FYC 91/2Y	Nether Stowey, Wellington
	Bedford TKG/Saxon	A620 OYA	Yeovil

A house fire is attended by a Ford/HCB-Angus Water Ladder.

Designs alter according to local requirements, as is illustrated by Lanca-shire County Fire Brigade who specified Water Ladders with provision for 220 gallons (1,000 litres) of water instead of the more common 400 gallons (1,800 litres). Delivered during the early 1980s, these Bedford Elricco KG-chassised machines carried CFE bodywork.

PUMP ESCAPES/WATER TENDER ESCAPES

Once very popular in urban areas, these machines carry a wheeled escape ladder on a Pump Escape fire engine, but with the advent of 45-ft (13.5 m) extension ladders, the number of wheeled escapes fell. There were 349 such machines in England and Wales during 1976, this dropping to under seventy in 1985 at a time when some 1,900 13.5 m ladders were in use. Examples of brigades with Pump Escapes/Water Tender Escapes are:

Brigade	Model	Registration (Year)	Comments
East Sussex	Dennis	WCD 783Y	Preston Circus
Hertfordshire	Dennis RS130	SPM 139/41X (1981)	Stevenage; Hemel Hempstead.
	AEC/Merryweather	NNK 103/4H (1970)	'A' and 'B' Division Spares
Isle of Man	Dennis F.35	999 CMN (1968)	Douglas
	Dennis F.38	999 GMN (1967)	Ramsey
West Yorkshire	Dennis	MNW 388L	Leeds (Reserve)

Kent Fire Brigade was the first British brigade to dispense with wheeled escapes in 1956, while Strathclyde Fire Brigade took the last operational wheeled escape off the run in 1983, following thirteen years' service at Port Glasgow and Rothesay. Hertfordshire's Watford Fire Station acquired a Water Tender Escape during 1984, fleet number W619.

Wheeled Escape in use (right).

MULTI-PURPOSE APPLIANCES

The mid-1970s witnessed an interesting innovation when Multi-Purpose vehicles were introduced, these machines being intended to deal with most emergencies. The early vehicles came with 400 gallons of water and, in addition to normal fire fighting equipment, they carried stretchers, blankets, emergency lighting, power tools and lifting gear. Devon Fire Brigade had some Commer Commando/HCB-Angus appliances of this type while conversions were carried out in brigade workshops on appliances mounted on

Devon Fire Brigade has several examples of Multi Purpose Vehicles such as this 1976 machine from Bampton, whose call sign, 35.1, is visible on the door.

No HGV licence is required to drive this Dodge RG08/ Carmichael appliance.

Bedford Chassis. Chief Fire Officer Harvey in 1975 described the Multi-Purpose machines as 'five in one' fire engines—Pump Escape, Pump, Water Tender, Foam Tender and Emergency Tender.

SMALLER PUMPING MACHINES

Standard Water Tender equipment including either a 35-ft or 45-ft ladder and four BA sets can be accommodated on smaller, lightweight fire appliances such as those based on Ford 'A' series chassis in use with Cumbria County Fire Service. The late 1970s saw this brigade receive several of these machines whose overall length of 19 ft 7 in and width of 7 ft makes them ideal for narrow lanes and fast acceleration.

More recently the HCB-Angus Midi Water Tender came on the market, based on a Bedford chassis measuring only 7 ft 3 in wide and carrying equipment similar to that found on larger Water Tenders. This machine is virtually a type 'B' Water Tender with 200 gallons (909 litres) of water and a crew of six, the gross weight of the vehicle being below the legal requirement for an HGV licence. Similar appliances on Dodge chassis can be found with Cumbria Fire Service. Smaller pumping machines operate in industrial and works' brigades, based on a variety of chassis including Ford Transit and the Ford 'A' series'. The Department of the Environment, for instance, introduced a Land Rover/Carmichael light fire appliance at Windsor Castle, this machine carrying a 90-gallon first aid tank, Godiva pump and two hose reels each with 180 ft of first aid hose.

Local authority brigades who have received light four-wheeled drive vehicles often employ the Land Rover chassis, and these appliances are referred to as L4P (light four-wheel drive vehicle with pump), L4T (light four-wheel drive vehicle with hose reel), L4R (light four-wheel drive vehicle with rescue equipment) and L4V (light four-wheel drive vehicle).

Stationed at Harrold, Bedfordshire, the 1982 Land Rover/Pilcher Greene vehicle accommodates a crew of three, Godiva UMP 50 two stage pump and a 180 ft × ¾ in hose reel.

Range Rovers are found as small pumping appliances, sometimes equipped with a front-mounted pump and three axles, typified by one in service with Gwynedd Fire Brigade.

Some examples of recent acquisitions are shown:

Brigade	Model	Registration	Comments
Bedfordshire	L/R Pilcher Greene L4P	DBN 537X	Harrold
Cornwall	Land Rover L4T	SGL 771/6Y	Replacing L4Ps at some stations
Cheshire	Land Rover Safari/ Jennings	DMB 901/8X	To eight stations
Gwent	Land Rover/ Saxon L4P	PHB 644/5/7Y	Usk, Cefn Fforest Abercarn
Leicestershire	Land Rover/HCB-Angus	BUT 906Y	Three axles, front-mounted pump

One of Gwent Fire Brigade's recently acquired Land Rover/Saxon L4Ps based at Abercarn Fire Station.

In rural areas where local conditions demand all-terrain, four-wheel drive vehicles, retained fire stations often have a Land Rover to back up the Water Ladders especially in cases where access is difficult for the larger

An interesting 6 × 6 pumping machine offering fire-fighting and rescue capabilities, received by Leicestershire Fire Service in the early 1980s.

machine, with many of these smaller vehicles carrying BA sets or rescue gear in addition to firefighting equipment. To illustrate this, one can usefully refer to retained fire stations accommodating Land Rover appliances plus Water Ladders or Water Tenders.

Brigade	Model	Registration	Comments
Clwyd	Dennis WrL	LJC 488R	Abergele
	Land Rover L4P	MEY 839R	
Hampshire	Bedford TK/Hampshire FB WrT	VTR 120T	Romsey
	Dennis 'D'/Jaguar/ Hampshire FB WrL	OAA 995L	
	Land Rover/Hampshire FB L4P	KPX 239P	
Somerset	Bedford TK/HCB-Angus WrL	PYC 321L	Burnham on Sea
	Bedford TKG/HCB-Angus WrT	KYC 871V	
	Land Rover/Somerset FB L4V (Cliff Rescue Unit)	UYD 587M	
West Sussex	Dennis 'D'WrL	CBP 86L	Storrington
	Dennis 'D' WrL	CPO 634L	
	Land Rover L4T	XOT 141V	

AERIAL APPLIANCES

TURNTABLE LADDERS

The Turntable Ladder consists of a long steel ladder comprising one main and three or four extensions extended by steel cable, most ladders reaching 100 ft (30.5 m). The ladder assembly is positioned at the rear of a heavy

South Yorkshire County Fire Service owns this Dennis F125/Carmichael/Magirus DL 30U Turntable Ladder.

chassis above the back axle and power for operating the ladder comes from the appliance's road engine. Some Turntable Ladders come with a pump, this model being termed a Turntable Ladder Pump. Turntable Ladders are usually stationed in built up areas containing high buildings, and a popular refinement is the fitting of a cage at the head of the ladder to facilitate rescues and to provide a platform for general firefighting.

The first British TL with rescue cage control was demonstrated by Merryweather in London during 1975; the 100 ft ladder could be elevated from minus 17 to plus 75 degrees. An all-British totally self-contained TL was launched in 1982 by Merryweather, aided by hydraulic consultants and Government sponsorship.

Turntable Ladders come with a variety of chassis and ladder makes, some quite old and still operational.

Brigade	Model	Registration (Year)	Comments
Cambridgeshire	Iveco/Carmichael/ Magirus	A621 SEW	Cambridge
Essex	Shelvoke and Drewry/ G&T/Merryweather	A344 MVX	Chelmsford
Humberside	Dennis DF/Dennis/ Magirus	ERH 679Y	Grimsby Central
Isle of Man	AEC/Mercury/ Merryweather	5724 MN (1962)	Douglas
Merseyside	Dennis F125/Dennis/ Merryweather	DWM 603Y	Southport
South Yorkshire	Dennis F125/ Carmichael/Magirus DL 30U	PHL 331X	Erskine Road, Rotherham
Tayside	ERF TL	JTS 720G (1969)	Perth
	AEC TL	MTS 279 (1961)	Strathmore Avenue
West Yorkshire	AEC/Merryweather	NWY 491E	Cleckheaton
	Dennis/Magirus	CWY 157Y	Huddersfield
Wiltshire	AEC/Mercury/ Merryweather	MMR 217G	Salisbury
	Dodge/Carmichael/ Magirus	XMW 758T	Swindon

The importance of having a Turntable Ladder on the run is underlined by the way in which Merryweather loan a TL to authorities whilst their own models are rechassised or overhauled. The former City of Plymouth TL (VJY 44) with another set of ladders may be observed up and down the country acting in this capacity.

An interesting trend in recent years has been the introduction of new foreign components to the range of UK Turntable Ladders. For customers who require a compact model, the Carmichael/Riffaud EPA 24 80 ft TL is ideal, with weight and dimensions very close to standard Water Tender's. Guernsey Fire Brigade owns a Ford/Camiva TL, manufactured in 1981, whose firefighting ladder height is 80 ft, and which can negotiate the narrow lanes found on the island. A MAN/Metz TL was ordered by Staffordshire in 1983 while Grampian Brigade runs a Scania LB 81H/Metz DL 30K TL, delivered late 1981, registration sso 66x. In the 1984/85 Financial Year a MAN 6D 240/Angloco/Metz TL went on the run at Preston Circus fire station, East Sussex. The registration is A210 CYJ.

Among recent disposals of Turntable Ladders one can refer to the ERF/Merryweather (CNM 455T) with Bedfordshire Fire Brigade, first registered in 1962, and extensively re-chassised and refurbished during 1982. When sold in 1984, the machine had travelled only 16,000 miles. Around the same period, West Midlands Fire Service disposed of their 1963 AEC/Merryweather Turntable Ladder, while during 1983–84 Lancashire sold the AEC/Merryweather TL (RRN 999) and the Morecambe-based Bedford/Merryweather TL (BTB 292E).

HYDRAULIC PLATFORMS

Hydraulic Platforms comprise two or three booms hinged together, the lower boom mounted on a turntable positioned above the rear axle of the chassis. A platform is located at the top of the upper boom or on an extension arm fitted to it, the platform mounted in such a way that the floor is always parallel to the chassis, irrespective of the angle of the booms. Simon Snorkels (Dudley) are the inventors and patentees of the three-boom system by which Simon Snorkels can go up, over and down the other side of an obstruction. A unit called the Super Snorkel was launched by Simon Engineering, Dudley, UK in 1984. It doubles the height of the largest existing Simon Snorkel. The new model has a towering upwards reach of 61.5 metres (202 feet) and a horizontal reach of 22 metres (72 feet).

United Kingdom brigades have several sizes of Hydraulic Platforms, smaller ones reaching heights of 40 to 50 ft (13.7 to 15.2 m) while larger ones can function at 65 to 75 ft (19.8 to 22.9 m) and 100 to 110 ft (30.5 to 33.5 m). During 1982, fire authorities received a revised specification for 65 to 75 ft Hydraulic Platforms, and one for Turntable Ladders (without cage) was issued to fire authorities in 1983. Hydraulic Platforms with booster pumps

An interesting view of an ERF Hydraulic Platform chassis and booms.

are referred to as HPPs, some pumping models carrying between 200 and 300 gallons (909 and 1364 litres) of water. Large amounts of water can be directed on to a fire through a monitor attached to the cage or, alternatively, through lines of hose, while the cage may be employed for rescue purposes.

A consideration of Hydraulic Platforms purchased in recent years highlights the variety of models available; Greater Manchester County Fire Service now operates Shelvoke and Drewry/Angloco/Simon SS263 models (BVM 543/4Y) and one can locate a Dennis F125/Dennis/Simon SS263 (ACM 413X) at Merseyside County Fire Brigade's Exmouth Street Fire Station. A re-chassised vehicle may be discovered at Bridgend (Mid-Glamorgan), incorporating a number of components; the registration of the Dodge G16/Angloco/Simon 85 ft machine is MTH 27X. Warwickshire Fire and Rescue Service have based a Shelvoke and Drewry/HCB-Angus/Simon 91 ft at Leamington Spa (DVC 274Y).

Just as brigades operate older Turntable Ladders, so too one can find instances of Hydraulic Platforms dating from the early 1970s:

The advantages of an Hydraulic Platform are clear at this accident.

Brigade	Model	Registration (Year)	Comments
Avon	Dodge K1050/ Simon 26 m	FHY 197K (1973)	Station CI
Greater Manchester	ERF SS 85	BTD 719J (1970)	Reserve
Gwent	Ford/HCB-Angus/ HPP 50 ft	AWO 674K (1971)	Self-contained 300 gpm pump
Hertfordshire	ERF HPP 70 ft	LJH 71L (1973)	Spare 'A' Division
Norfolk	ERF/Simon SS 70 ft	FNG 779K (1971)	King's Lynn
West Sussex	ERF/Simon	MPX 842J (1971)	Worthing
West Yorkshire	ERF/Simon 70 ft	VHL 526J (1970)	Wakefield

The Shelvoke and Drewry/Carmichael/Bronto lift appliance.

Some United Kingdom manufacturers have expressed an interest in hydraulic access platforms from overseas, one intriguing combination being a Shelvoke and Drewry/Carmichael/Bronto Lift, the last component normally associated with Sisu fire chassis in Finland. Cleveland Fire Brigade has a Shelvoke and Drewry/Carmichael/Bronto 322 based at Hartlepool (A999 HAJ).

Moving to recent disposals of Hydraulic Platforms, the 1972 Dodge K1050 with Orbitor 72 ft Hydraulic Platform was sold by Royal Berkshire Fire Brigade during 1984, and Humberside Fire Brigade's AEC/Simon SS 65 ft HP at Bransholme was replaced the previous year. Durham County Fire Brigade sold the 1974 Dennis F48 Pump/50 ft Simon SS 50 HP in 1984 (RUP 529M), this vehicle having covered almost 17,000 miles.

The early 1980s witnessed the sale of a 1972 ERF 84 PFS/HCB-Angus/ Simon 50 ft owned by Cambridgeshire Fire and Rescue Service, registration SUE 668K, while 1984 saw Greater Manchester County Fire Service dispose of an ERF/SS (FTJ 410F) Hydraulic Platform appliance.

SIMONITORS

The 'Simonitor' was developed by Simons of Dudley during early 1970s, featuring a telescopic boom similar in principle to a telescopic crane. Positioned at the head of the boom was a monitor which could be directed remotely from the ground without requiring a fireman to operate the boom from its head.

Greater Manchester County Fire Service kept an ERF Firefighter TSM 15 on the run until the early 1980s, registration YVU 133M, acquired during

Shown in the former Manchester Fire Brigade livery, this 1974 Simonitor was built on an ERF chassis.

1974 along with two similar vehicles from Lancashire County Fire Brigade following the reorganisation of fire authorities.

The County of Clwyd Fire Brigade operates a Simonitor from the retained fire station at Flint, this particular marque being a Dennis F48/Dennis/Simon TSM 15, registration SDM 391M, while Essex County Fire Brigade maintains Dennis F48 Simonitors at Basildon and Grays, AVW 980L (1973) and MAR 799P (1975).

Durham County Fire Brigade sold its 1974 Dennis F48/Pump 50 ft Simon TSM 15 Simonitor appliance, RUP 530M in 1984, the machine having done 17,250 miles.

ROAD ACCIDENT VEHICLES

Fire brigades are always improving the equipment carried on Water Tenders and Water ladders, but at some incidents extra rescue/cutting equipment may be needed, in which case a Road Accident Vehicle (RAV) will be sent on. These vehicles appear in a variety of guises and a Range Rover base is often employed, especially when the close proximity of motorways demands rapid deployment of road accident appliances. In many cases the Rescue Tender/Emergency Tenders (below) may carry out the function of RAVs.

Now operating with Gwynedd Fire Brigade at Holyhead and classed as a Rescue Pump, the Range Rover/Carmichael vehicle is seen here in Anglesey Fire Brigade livery before the reorganisation of fire authorities.

The types of road rescue tenders may be observed on considering a selection of brigades:

Brigade	Model	Registration (Year)	Comments
Cheshire	Range Rover/ Carmichael Rescue Tender	DMB 67/8S	Knutsford; Birchwood
Durham	Bedford RAV	6249 PT	Newton Aycliffe
East Sussex	Jeep 6 × 4/Angloco	A778/9 EPN	Uckfield, Battle
Gwynedd	Range Rover/ Carmichael Res P	TEY 188L	Holyhead
Hampshire	Dodge W400/ HCB-Angus	BTP 486W	Aldershot
Humberside	Reynolds Boughton RB 44 Apollo/ Merryweather	A 319 NRH	Grimsby, Cl
Lincolnshire	Bedford/Fulton & Wylie	A 648 7FE	Stamford
Northamptonshire	Ford 'A'/Smith	VNV 338/9W	Northampton, Wellingborough
North Yorkshire	Ford/Angloco	MAJ 106W (1981)	Northallerton
Warwickshire	Bedford/HCB-Angus	HWK 999N (1975)	Nuneaton
Wiltshire	Range Rover/ Carmichael	KMR 673P	Chippenham

Rescue vehicles carry a comprehensive range of equipment demonstrated by that carried on each of the five Ford 'A' Series rescue vehicles in North Yorkshire Fire Brigade.

Some of the equipment carried on Ford 'A' Series Rescue Vehicles in North Yorkshire Fire Brigade, which has five such appliances in service, received between 1978 and 1981.

Cab			Nearside Rear			Rear Locker	
Log books	4		BA Hose reel and drum	1		Loud hailer	1
Reflective jackets	2		Radiac dosimeters	10		Large axes	2
Message pad	1		Radiac gloves (*pairs*)	10		Police accident signs	2
Nominal roll tally and			Radiac contamination			Tripods	6
pencil	1		meter	1		Air lifting bags	2
Maps	13		Radiac survey meter	1		Air lifting bag control	2
Hazard Industries Book	1		Radiac equipment box	1		Halogen floodlight,	
BCF Extinguisher	1		BA Waist belt lines	2		110 volt	4
Hazard Information						Floodlights, 240 volt	4
Board	1		**Nearside Rear**			Extension cables and	
Entonox	1		GP Line, 100 ft	1		reels	4
Teesside Airport			GP Line, 50 ft (15 m)	1		Honda generators	2
Disaster Plan	1		BA Guideline	1		Kango generator	1
			BA Control jacket	1		Spade	1
Traverse Locker			BA Main Control Board	1		Shovel	1
Stretcher	1		BA Stage II Board	1		Bottle jack and handle	2
First Aid Kit	1		BA Guide line tallies (*set*)	1		Trolley jack and handle	1
Brooms	2		CABA Sets complete	2		GP saws	2
Blankets	3		Communications			Quick release knife and	
Gauntlets (*pairs*)	4		equipment	1		sheath	1
Bardic Torch	1		Leather blanket	1		Bardic lamps	2
Cable Slings	2					Bolt croppers	1
'T' Keys	2		**Offside Rear**			Toolkit, box and	
Blue flashing lamps	2		Railway warning horns	2		padlock	1
Leather gloves (*pairs*)	4		Blue flashing lamps	4		Funnel	1
Ground Anchor	1		Cengar saws	2		Oil can	1
Ground Anchor Stakes	12		Zip guns	2		Black Hawk Hydraulic	
Sledge Hammer	1		Air Line, 10 ft (3 m)	5		Equipment	2
DP Extinguisher	1		Air Line, 20 ft (6 m)	1		Petrol can, 2-gallon	1
Tirfor and handles	2		BA Air packs with			Hydraulic oil container	1
Tirfor cable, 60 ft			cylinders	2		Amber flashing lamp	1
(18 m)	1		Abrasive cutter	1		Small axes with pouch	
Tirfor cable, 30 ft (9 m)	1		Spare discs	4		and strap	2
Snatch blocks	2		Spanners for disc cutter	2		Cones	14
Tirfor chains			Ram, 20-ton	1		Crow bar	1
Wheel chocks set	1		Body cutter	1		Gas tight suits	4
BA Cylinders	30		Air Line 'T' Pieces	2			
Rubber gloves (*pairs*)	2		Cengar oil (tin)	1		Air lines BA	4
Salvage sheets	3		Protective goggles	4			
Shackles			Ear defenders	4			
Skid chains	1						
BA Cylinder test gauge	1		**Roof**				
			Triple extension ladder	1			
			Halogen floodlights,				
			500 watts	2			

EMERGENCY TENDERS

These vehicles carry multifarious items of equipment designed for firefighting and for rescue and life saving purposes generally. Typical gear would include generators for providing lighting and power for tools, heavy lifting and spreading equipment, lifting bags and resuscitation facilities.

Some of the road traffic accident work is now carried out by faster Road Accident Vehicles (RAV) or Rapid Intervention Vehicles (RIV), but brigades still purchase the larger Emergency Tenders whose equipment is invaluable at certain incidents. It is clear that specialist machines have more than one rôle; for instance, Shropshire Fire Service Ford/CFE machines (WUX 348S and UUJ 724S) are termed Emergency Tenders, yet their comprehensive rescue gear means that they also act as Road Accident Vehicles.

Emergency Tenders are built on a variety of chassis and consequently vary in size, as the following table shows.

Brigade	Model	Registration	Comments
Cleveland	Dennis R	DAJ 700T	Stockton
Devon	Dodge G12/ Angloco	A975 NDV	Torquay
Durham	Dennis	MPT 743P	Peterlee
Greater Manchester	Dodge/Hestair Eagle	WBA 546S	Lisburne Lane
Lothian and Borders	Dodge S56/ Mountain Range	NSX 359Y	MacDonald Road
Merseyside	Dennis RS 133 ET/CU	DWM 605Y	Exmouth Street (front-mounted winch)
Norfolk	Bedford/ Carmichael	PEX 669W	Norwich
Shropshire	Ford 'A' Series/CFE	UUJ 724S	Shrewsbury
West Yorkshire	Ford A0610/Anglo	CWY 154/6Y	Wetherby, Cleckheaton, Keighley
Wiltshire	Dodge/Carmichael	FHR 622W	Trowbridge

A Dodge/Hestair Eagle Emergency Tender attending a major incident.

Emergency Tenders are frequently called out when a job may necessitate servicing of BA sets, a control point or extra lighting, and, consequently, the predetermined attendance at places like hospitals or airports will include Emergency Tenders in addition to Water Ladders and other appliances. Several brigades operate Road Accident Vehicles alongside the larger Emergency Tenders, West Yorkshire Fire Service being an example of an authority which refers to both categories as 'Emergency Tenders', seen on examining three of the six Divisions:

Division in West Yorkshire	Station	Model	Registration (Year)
Bradford	Idle	Ford	WWR 659S (1978)
	Keighley	Land Rover	SWX 277L (1972)
Calderdale	Halifax	Ford	DUB 801T (1979)
Kirklees	Huddersfield	Ford	DUB 802T (1979)

SALVAGE TENDERS

Following fires where damage to stock is likely from water and smoke, it is essential to offer some sort of protection. The Salvage Corps carried out such work until they were disbanded in 1984 and fire brigades are now acquiring vehicles which carry specialist salvage equipment including salvage sheets, extractor fans and brooms.

Salvage Tenders either operate exclusively in this rôle or may be a combined Emergency Tender/Salvage Tender (EST) manned by personnel who have training in salvage operations. Cheshire Fire Brigade is an example of an authority possessing a Salvage Tender, a Ford 'A' Series

An interesting scene of a job attended by a Salvage Corps Damage Control Unit and a Ford 'A' Series Salvage Tender (DTU 347S) from Cheshire Fire Brigade, based at A5 Winsford.

diesel model, acquired during 1978 (DTU 347S), while among Greater Manchester County Fire Service's fleet one finds further instances of Salvage Tenders in the Ford D1114s, ANC 777T (1978) and TBA 260R (1977) stationed at Bury and Hyde.

CHEMICAL INCIDENT UNITS

Chemical Incident Units attend jobs where extra material and manpower is required when fires/spillages involving chemicals occur. The CIUs carry a variety of gear including decontamination equipment and extra protective clothing. Somerset Fire Brigade's CIU comes on a Ford Transit chassis with Brigade bodywork (KYA 428N, 1975) and is based at Bridgwater. Norfolk Fire Service operates a Dodge/HCB-Angus CIU (SUF 795N) from Sprowston Fire Station, which also accommodates a Dennis Water Ladder (UCL 493W). Gloucestershire Fire and Rescue Service has a relatively new Chemical Unit in its Dodge G75 vehicle stationed at Stroud (CDG 998Y), while the Highland and Islands Fire Brigade's unit is found at Inverness, built on a Ford chassis, LAS 160Y. Gwent Fire Brigade employs a 1972 Dennis vehicle as Chemical Incident Unit, registration WDW 202K.

Personnel from Norfolk Fire Service demonstrate some of the equipment carried on the Brigade's Chemical Incident Unit.

CONTROL UNITS

When large incidents require centralised control on the fireground a Control Unit is usually sent to set up a communication link between the job and the brigade control room. The Control Units vary in design but generally have field telephones, maps and facilities for senior officers to hold meetings, and can usually transmit and receive on any of the main scheme VHF channels.

During 1977, London Fire Brigade received an interesting Control Unit, having a Willowbrook single-deck coachbody shell mounted on a Ford R1014 chassis with Angloco components. Greater Manchester County Fire Service sends an articulated unit (TU) to larger incidents when a Control Unit is needed, while smaller examples can be seen in the Ford A01610/Angloco operated by West Yorkshire Fire Service (VWR 821X) and the Ford A0609/Benson model in service with Humberside Fire Brigade.

There are many examples of vehicles having a dual rôle, for example, Leicestershire Fire Service's two Emergency Tender/Control Units are built on Dodge Commando RG13 chassis with Angloco body, the control unit area having room for two radio operators seated at individual work areas. The appliances were allocated to Leicester and Loughborough in 1982 (VUT 311X, VUT 312X).

During 1983, Bedfordshire Fire Service received Control Units manned by control room staff who attend larger incidents in the Bedford CF350 demountable units.

A combined Emergency Tender/Control Unit with Leicestershire Fire Service.

Control Room staff are transported to major jobs in Control Units with Bedfordshire Fire Service.

FOAM TENDERS

When large amounts of foam are required at incidents, brigades will despatch their Foam Tender (FoT) or Foam Trailer (FoTr). Typical examples are seen in the Dennis FoT on the run with Hereford and Worcester Fire Brigade, carrying up to 6800 litres of foam (HAB 900X). A Dodge G13 Commando 2/Carmichael machine, holding 600 gallons of foam compound and fitted with a Godiva 1,000 gallons per minute pump, is a popular Foam Tender, exemplified by the model with Esso Petroleum's Fire Brigade.

Some United Kingdom brigades adapt older vehicles for the purpose of Foam Tender duties, instanced by a Norfolk Fire Service Foam Salvage Tender based at Great Yarmouth; this is a former Water Ladder and was put on the run during 1982 (HPW 412L), featuring components from Ford 'D' and ERF machines plus the Brigade's modifications. Similarly, the former Bedford/HCB-Angus Emergency Tender from Cornwall County Fire Brigade's Bodmin Station (NRL 385F) was converted into an FoT by the Brigade and stationed at Falmouth in 1983, Cornwall disposing of a 1961 Austin 4-ton Foam Tender the same year (233 NAF).

This Dodge/Carmichael Foam Tender holds 600 gallons of foam compound and is in service with Esso Petroleum's Fire Brigade.

The Amoco refinery blaze at Milford Haven brought thirteen Foam Tenders together in addition to 45 Pumps and six Hydraulic Platforms. Two Foam Tenders came from Dyfed, the rest from West Glamorgan, South Glamorgan, Avon and Gwent Fire Brigades, together with one each from Texaco, Gulf, BP and Amoco refinery brigades.

WATER CARRIERS

Water Carriers are found in several brigades and are used when water supplies at a job need to be supplemented. The vehicles are often former oil tankers, although some are bought new. Capacities vary and appliances carry both audible and visible warning devices for use when proceeding to incidents. An interesting combination of rôle is observed in the two Dodge/Angloco Water Carriers/Foam Tenders operated by Bedfordshire Fire Service, based at Kempston (XRO 614S) and Toddington (XRO 615S).

The Isle of Wight County Fire Brigade has three Water Carriers, at Newport, East Cowes and Freshwater, built on Ford DD and Bedford TKM chassis and manned by whole-time and retained crews. Guernsey

An interesting combined Water Carrier/Foam Tender (XRO 614S) alongside a 1978 Dodge appliance attending a large incident in Bedfordshire.

Fire Brigade's Ford Water Carrier was manufactured in 1976, accommodating a crew of two, a 500 gallons per minute fire pump and 1,000 gallons of water, while Hampshire Fire Brigade introduced an interesting model during 1983 (UTP 78K), based on a former Dennis F108/HFB Pump Escape and stationed at Fordingbridge, and replacing the Bedford TK model (HOR 208E). During the same year, Derbyshire Fire Service placed a Dennis DF Water Carrier at Chesterfield (ACH 449Y). Among disposals of vehicles, one can refer to the 1967 Water Carrier in service with Cambridgeshire Fire and Rescue Service (HVE 939F), a Bedford 4 × 4 sold in 1984.

HOSE LAYERS

Hose Layers can be employed to augment the supply of water available for firefighting since they are designed and equipped to enable long lengths of hose to be laid out at speed. Many of these appliances have up to one mile (1.6 km) of hose which is so carried on the lorry as to enable it to be paid out while the vehicle travels at speeds of up to 20 mph (32 km/h). Humberside received a Hose Layer on a Ford Cargo chassis during the 1984/85 financial year, replacing the Bedford/AFS model (NYV 627) based at C4 Immingham. Other instances of Hose Layers include:

Brigade	Model	Registration	Comments
Avon	Bedford/Oldland Bodywork	EHW 747K	Station A2, received 1971
Isle of Man	Dennis F8	PBN 72	Foam Tender/Hose Layer
Merseyside	Ford A0910/MCFB	DMB 721X	HL/WU—St Helens

DEMOUNTABLE UNITS

The problem of supplying special appliances, especially for infrequent incidents, encouraged the development of a new genre of body systems during the mid-1970s. Following initial work by brigades such as Mid Glamorgan Fire Service, a system was devised using a hydraulic lifting and securing mechanism powered from a standard power take-off mounted either on a new chassis or a conversion of an existing chassis. Bodies can be loaded according to the incident's requirements, and today one finds a variety of Demountable Units as portrayed by the range of 'Pods' or 'Units' received by Oxfordshire Fire Service during 1980–81. Eight purpose-built bodies were constructed for use with the three 'Nova lift' equipped chassis, the Pods incorporating a Hose Layer, Control Unit, Decontamination Unit, Foam Tender, Canteen Van, Emergency Salvage, Breathing Apparatus Tender and General-Purpose flatbed lorry. Royal Berkshire Fire Brigade has an interesting Pod Foam Tender, interchangeable with a BA Tender/Salvage Tender based at Langley, with foam carried in a compartmented tank of 1,020 gallons, while, in 1983, Nottinghamshire County Fire Brigade introduced a mobile education and exhibition centre based on the Powell Duffryn 'Rolonof Two' System, the first such vehicle to be put in operation by a United Kingdom fire brigade.

Nottinghamshire's mobile education and exhibition centre demounted from the truck on arrival at a site and telescopically extended to double effectively the internal space area.

Recent trends would suggest an increase in the number of recipients of Pods/Demountable Units, exemplified by acquisitions during 1983–84, when Bedfordshire Fire Service installed Control Units/Chemical Incident Unit Pods at Luton and Kempston, and Gwent Fire Brigade's Dodge/Carmichael Foam Tender (KTX 595D) was converted to a Demountable appliance with a 'Ratcliffe Cantilever' at the rear.

The financial year 1984/85 brought a new concept of the charging of breathing apparatus cylinders on site when South Glamorgan Fire Brigade introduced a Pod similar in appearance to a shipping container. The container accommodates a BA compressor for charging purposes, control room and a workshop area.

BREATHING APPARATUS TENDERS

When breathing apparatus sets need servicing on station or when an incident necessitates extensive use of breathing apparatus sets, brigades may send a unit which can recharge, service, repair or clean the sets; these vehicles are frequently known as Breathing Apparatus Tenders. Some are purpose-built, but others are adapted from existing machines, such as the BAT which came into service with Warwickshire Fire and Rescue Service during 1983, a Ford Transit/WFRS vehicle which had served as a Foam Salvage Tender and Emergency Tender (SWD 238G) and is now based at Kenilworth. Cheshire Fire Brigade owns a Ford 'A' Series (A0609) model received in 1978 (DTU 346S), while West Sussex Fire Brigade operates units from stations at Worthing (Ford, CPO 635L), and Horsham (Ford, CPO 636L).

RECOVERY VEHICLES

Various brigades employ Heavy Recovery Vehicles for use by brigade workshops who may wish to tow or lift vehicles from the fleet, while certain authorities have Recovery Vehicles/Cranes whose main task would be to assist at road traffic accidents where heavy lifting gear is required.

Some examples of brigades who have workshop Recovery Vehicles are West Midlands Fire Service and Derbyshire Fire Service, the former authority introducing a hybrid model to its fleet in 1982. Using an old Dudley Fire and Ambulance Service 70 ft Hydraulic Platform with ERF 84RS chassis as a base, brigade workshops in West Midlands Fire Service converted the HCB-Angus-bodied appliance to a Recovery Vehicle for brigade workshops and today PFD 777F is operational in red livery. West Midlands sold two Recovery Vehicles in 1983–84—a 1962 Bedford (ex-Home Office) and a 1965 Dennis 'F' machine.

Derbyshire Fire Service had a Bedford Recovery Vehicle (ex-AFS) which was built in 1962; this was replaced in 1985. The former Berkshire and Reading Fire Brigade employed a Commer 'QX'/Markham Breakdown Emergency Tender until 1974 as a workshop's Recovery Vehicle, which featured a rear mounted 'Harvey Frost' Crane; it was replaced by the present ET/HRV.

Brigade workshops in Cheshire Fire Brigade have a Bedford MUR 156 in/ Reynolds Boughton 6-ton light Recovery Unit for towing fire appliances while an interesting marque in heavy rescue vehicles was observed until recently in Gloucestershire Fire and Rescue Service's 1967 AEC Marshall vehicle carrying Bates bodywork and a Holmes crane (KDF 146E). Based at Stroud until 1983, the appliance was replaced by a Dodge 50 series 'automatic'/Carmichael Rescue Unit (JHY 616X).

Surrey County Fire Brigade's 1960 Breakdown/Recovery Truck comes with a Thornycroft Nubian 6 × 6 chassis and a rear-mounted twin-winch crane lifting 5 tons, power for the machine received from a Rolls-Royce B-81 engine.

A further Recovery/Breakdown Vehicle to be considered, the 1970 Dennis Maxim-Holmes machine (DHN 999J) stationed at Darlington, moved into

The Bedford/Reynolds Boughton Recovery Unit comes with an 18,000-lb capacity UM16 mechanical salvage winch, while the jib has two position stays for carrying loads and for suspended tows.

Durham County Fire Brigade in 1974 from the County Borough of Darlington Fire Brigade. This machine is employed for some recovery work and is available on request for heavy vehicle accidents.

OTHER VEHICLES

Many fire brigades utilise General Purpose Lorries (GPL) for various tasks such as transporting materials from workshops to fire stations or for carrying extra gear to incidents. Cleveland County Fire Brigade has a Ford GPL (KAJ 556W) stationed at Middlesbrough, while Cornwall County Fire Brigade sold a 1962 Austin GPL (FGK 80) in the early 1980s.

When protracted jobs lead to the provision of refreshments for fire personnel, brigades will send a Canteen Van. Some of these vehicles are based on Demountable Units/Pods, but others appear in a variety of guises. For instance, Hertfordshire Fire Brigade owns a Ford Transit Canteen Van, which is based at Welwyn Garden City (GVD 269N), Staffordshire Fire Brigade favours a 1967 Commer 'Walk-Through' (DRF 590S), based at Stafford, while a 1980 Dodge (TTJ 317V) is found in Merseyside County Fire Brigade. Conversions of vehicles for Canteen Van purposes are in evidence, like Cleveland County Fire Brigade's model—a former Ford 'A' mobile workshop (TDC 869K) altered to a Canteen Van and put on the run in 1984.

Some larger authorities possess Trailer/Tractor Units, these articulated machines appearing in such rôles as the Operational Support Units (OSU) observed in Greater Manchester County Fire Service as mobile control rooms. Here one finds a number of appliances including the Altrincham based Dodge OSU (AND 406T) which has gear similar to that found on an Emergency Tender, like a 100-ton ram and two 'hi-ex' foam generators, with other machines located at Pendlebury (PNB 480W), Bolton (AND 409T) and Blackley (GNE 709V).

Personnel Carrying Vehicles are commonplace in Britain's fire brigades,

Acting as a Control Unit, the Dodge Trailer/Tractor Unit (PNB 480W) is a valuable appliance at major incidents.

Royal Berkshire Fire Brigade, for instance, owning a Sherpa Crewbus (CTF 655V), Mid-Glamorgan Fire Service running a larger 45-seater Bedford coach, new in 1966.

Under the heading of Utility Vehicles one can refer to the Service Vans and Station Vans which appear in all brigades, these coming in a variety of forms, such as Escort, Transit, Marina or Leyland Sherpa Vans. Similarly, Staff Cars for officers are bought from several manufacturers, South Glamorgan County Fire Service possessing a number of cars, including a Vauxhall (EHB 241V) for 'A' Division, and Warwickshire Fire and Rescue Service having ten Ford Cortinas and a Granada Consort based at Brigade HQ, all received in 1979–80.

Petrol Carriers are found in some brigades and are used to convey fuel to certain incidents, where, for instance, portable pumps may need refuelling if used for a long time. Alternatively, cans of fuel may be transported to incidents in a General Purpose Lorry.

Instances of vehicles in use with only some brigades would include West Yorkshire Fire Service's Damage Control Unit, a Ford A0610/Anglo based at Bramley (VWR 820X) and the Photographic Unit and the Fire Investigation Unit with London Fire Brigade. The former is based on a 1979 Ford Cortina Estate (YHV 222T), the Investigation Unit coming in a 1979 Ford Transit van (YHV 232T). Staffordshire Fire Brigade brings out its 1964 Land Rover Snowplough (ERF 723B) when weather requires its use, and East Sussex Fire Brigade obtained a purpose-built Bedford 'M' Forest Fire Vehicle during 1984.

FIRE FIGHTING ON WATER

A number of Fire Brigades possess smaller Fire/Rescue Boats in the form of inshore rescue craft, some preferring larger vessels. London Fire Brigade, for example, operates the *Fire Swift* and *Fire Hawk*, received in 1975 and 1976 respectively. The craft have a gross tonnage of 18.74, and measure 13.7 m in length and 4.1 m in beam, with a draught of 1.07 m and displacement of 12 tons. Capable of achieving a speed of 17 knots, the vessels receive engine power from two 145 hp 6-cylinder Perkins Diesels and have two fire pumps each delivering 530 gallons per minute (2,636 litres per minute) at 4.2 kg/cm².

A larger Fire Boat can be found with Cleveland County Fire Brigade, this authority owning the Fire Boat *Cleveland Endeavour*, which has been in service some six years and whose impressive array of firefighting equipment incorporates four Merryweather dual-purpose monitors and an SS70/45 Simon Marine Snorkel which gives a working height of 55 ft (16.5 m) above water level. Interesting features of this craft are a two-bed hospital cabin which can be sealed and pressurised with compressed air for at least 30 minutes to enable the boat to leave the area safely, plus a sprinkler system with nozzles at 2 m intervals around the upper deck and superstructure. This protects the craft during firefighting operations when the two principal Merryweather pump sets can deliver up to 3,250 gallons (14,765 litres) per minute at 100 psi (7 bar); in addition to the main pump, there is a high pressure hose reel pump plus foam tanks.

Cleveland County Fire Brigade's Searider speeds to an incident.

1983 witnessed an addition to Cleveland Fire Brigade's fleet when an Avon Searider SR5M replaced an ex-MoD Gemini Inflatable Boat, the new craft being employed as a Tender/Rescue Craft with the *Cleveland Endeavour*. This latest boat is 4.05 m long with a 1.8 m beam, and can reach a speed in excess of 35 knots. It accommodates a crew of two plus ten passengers.

Moving to further examples of Fire/Rescue Craft one can refer to the Zodiac/Mercury 50 Inshore Rescue Craft in service with the States of Jersey Fire Service, while Greater Manchester County Fire Service owns an Inflatable Craft, received in 1977, which is towed to jobs by a Range Rover. The Fire Service in Jersey has operated Zodiac Inshore Rescue Boats since 1960 and claims to have pioneered the use of this type of craft not only within the British Fire Service but in advance of the Royal National Liftboat Institution.

PUMPING SYSTEMS FOR OFFSHORE FIRE FIGHTING

The Emergency Support Vessel *Iolair* (the name is Gaelic for Eagle) is operated by British Petroleum, and is the most advanced offshore Emergency Support Vessel in the world.

The vessel is fitted with Worthington-Simpson firefighting systems and engine room pumps. The firefighting system includes four main fire pumps and seventeen monitors which can deliver 13,600 tonnes of water per hour at a range of 200 m which is probably the longest throw of such a volume of water with a reliable 'footprint' of delivery, fitted to a firefighting vessel.

In addition to the firefighting system, Worthington-Simpson designed and supplied the drenching system for the purpose of allowing the vessel to approach the fire in a saturated state so that it will withstand the intense heat.

The *Iolair* was designed so that it could carry out its fully operational firefighting requirements during almost any weather conditions. For this purpose, the firefighting system was designed to include a small computer capable of integrating with the vessel's main computer thus enabling the movement of the large fire monitors to be computer controlled in accordance with the wave and weather conditions being experienced at any one time.

Delivering 13,600 tonnes of water per hour, the 'Iolair' provides valuable facilities for offshore firefighting in the mid-1980s.

5

Salvage Corps

The spring of 1984 witnessed the end of the Salvage Corps in London, Liverpool and Glasgow. They had worked in close association with local fire brigades, but were at the same time independent of the local fire authority. Many brigades now run Salvage Units and some of the Corps' vehicles and equipment operate in local authority livery, following the disbanding of the three United Kingdom Salvage Corps.

Following the Great Fire of London (1666), when damage estimated at almost £11 million was caused by the four-day conflagration, various fire insurance companies sought ways of preventing similar loss again. Company Fire Brigades were formed by insurance offices, each office providing a metal plate or fire mark to properties which they insured.

It became apparent to insurance companies that the very agent used by fire brigades, namely, water, was in itself forming an increasing percentage of the total fire loss figure, and the establishment of a Salvage Corps became a necessity.

During 1842, there were several disastrous fires in Liverpool, including a blaze in a Formby Street cotton warehouse which destroyed 48,000 bales of cotton insured for £384,000, the total loss being £700,000. Insurance companies raised their rates in the city and formed the Liverpool Salvage Corps. Similar corps were established in London (1866) and Glasgow (1873).

The Salvage Corps were run and maintained at their own expense by the member fire insurance companies and Lloyds with the principal aim of preventing damage to goods and property from fire and water, and, although the Corps worked alongside local fire brigades, they were completely independent of the local fire authority.

The main method adopted at extensive fires and at fires in private dwelling houses was the use of waterproof covers for the protection of merchandise, furniture, machinery, etc. Even when extinguishing water was carefully and efficiently applied, the use of these covers was a necessity and was remarkably effective if quickly put on and properly erected.

During the progress of the fire and while the fire brigade was carrying out firefighting operations, the work of the Corps included moving and covering contents with these sheets; diverting water by means of sheets slung from wall fixings or on specially designed rods; picking up carpets and other contents; clearing water off the floors by means of brooms, shovels and squeegees; damming doorways and other floor openings; opening up drains and keeping them clear within and outside the premises; ventilating the premises when the fire situation permits and the protecting of adjoining exposures—where there are broken windows or other uncovered openings, or outside stock. It was not usual to remove contents from a building which

London Salvage Corps rushing to an incident in 1918.

was on fire, but this was done, as far as time and manpower permitted, in the case of buildings or parts of buildings which were likely to be completely involved.

These were some of the main damage control steps taken during the fire and the measure of success of these operations depended entirely on speed of performance. The ideal damage control conditions existed when these operations could be tackled before or as soon as possible after extinguishing water had been applied.

Passageways were cut through the débris to facilitate drainage; wet floors covered with sawdust and, as soon as the water ceased to drip through the floors and ceilings, the waterproof sheets were removed to assist drying out. Dangerous building features of a minor nature, broken and loose slates, glass and plaster were removed and the buildings made as weatherproof as possible by covering windows and roofs with tarpaulins or roofing felt. This latter service afforded protection to both buildings and contents and is of special value when it makes it possible for occupation to be continued and business to be carried on.

Salvagemen worked a 42-hour week, providing a 24-hour service with operational members divided into four groups whose hours of duty worked on a rota system, each Corps having a Chief Salvage Officer in charge.

VEHICLES

Salvage Corps vehicles were equipped with blue flashing lights and two-tone horns and were recognised as emergency vehicles under the Road Traffic Act. Red in colour, the appliances had a white waist band and were equipped with two way radio communications.

The Damage Control Units carried the following gear: Plastic coated fabric salvage sheets, rolls of PVC drain guards, electric squeegee for mopping up water, electric smoke extraction fans, electrical submersible pump, electrically operated spray guns, cable reels, large electric drills, cartridge operated nail guns, petrol driven disc cutters, electric generators, compressor unit with spray gun, telescopic Acro props, high-powered lighting heads, sprinkler heads for replacement, corrugated iron and firefighting equipment.

The Corps also employed general purpose lorries, mobile cranes plus staff vans.

LIVERPOOL SALVAGE CORPS

Based in Derby Road, Liverpool Salvage Corps had some 26,000 calls a year in the early 1980s attended by one or more of its fleet:

Type and Use	Registration	Date Registered
Ford D0710 Damage Control Unit	OKA 70S	24.07.78
Ford D0710 Damage Control Unit	RKC 940T	12.12.78
Ford D0710 Damage Control Unit	TEM 476V	1.09.79
Bedford TL860 Damage Control Unit	EKF 395Y	1.09.82
Ford Transit (General Purpose)	VKC 723V	21.04.80
Bedford Luton Van (General Purpose)	ELV 455Y	13.12.82
Personnel Carrier	XBG 654W	16.12.80
Ford Escort 0-7 (Staff Car)	THF 574V	1.08.79
Chrysler (2-Litre-Deputy Chief Officer)	XFR 25V	22.01.80
Ford Cortina (Chief Officer)	XHF 185W	8.01.81

A principal factor influencing insurance companies when establishing the Liverpool Corps was the close proximity of Lancashire's cotton mills,

Pictured standing by at an incident, this Ford Damage Control Unit was acquired by the Liverpool Corps during 1978.

Casual labour was employed to remove soiled cotton following a fire.

Liverpool of course serving as the port of entry for cotton, much of which was stored in warehouses, awaiting transportation. Following a fire involving cotton, it was quite common in the 1940s and 1950s for casual labour to be brought in for the purpose of removing soiled and damaged cotton from bales. During World War Two, the Liverpool organisation carried out firefighting duties following enemy air raids and consequently saved vast amounts of cotton from destruction when the Corps reconditioned 26,000 bales of cotton from warehouses and 20,000 bales from ships.

The Liverpool Corps, in keeping with counterparts in London and Glasgow, responded not only to major fires in industrial and commercial premises but also to jobs in private houses when it was felt extra protection was required from water or when a roof might require a temporary salvage sheet in place to keep out the rain.

The Liverpool Corps operated beyond the confines of Merseyside, attending jobs as far afield as Wales, Newcastle under Lyme and Cheshire, and, in addition to serving the community, the Corps ran successful salvage courses for the local authority brigades of Avon, Humberside, West Yorkshire, North Yorkshire and Greater Manchester. An interesting move was made by the Merseyside County Council in the summer of 1984 when it decided to

National Fire Service Salvage Course under instruction in Liverpool during the 1940s.

finance the renamed Merseyside Salvage Corps. This would carry on until the end of 1985 when the situation would be reviewed. With some 40 men, the Corps provides a 24-hour service and will respond to anywhere in Britain.

GLASGOW SALVAGE CORPS

Formed in 1873, Glasgow Salvage Corps was the youngest and smallest of the United Kingdom's Corps. First stationed in Nicholas Street, it later moved to Albion Street and then progressed to its last premises at Maitland Street. Three principal appliances in use up to March 1984 were:

This Mercedes vehicle came into service with the Glasgow Corps in the mid-1970s.

The Bedford TK 860 Series/Fulton Wylie Damage Control Unit (MUS 920V).

Registration Numbers: BGB 901S, HHS 924T MUS 920V

Built On: Bedford TK 860 Series chassis and cab

Powered By: KD 330 Diesel Engine (5408 cc)

Front Cab: Built by Fulton and Wylie of Irvine. Front cabin extended to carry one officer, one driver and four men

Rear Body: Built by Fulton and Wylie of Irvine. Rear body built of aluminium containing two side lockers on driver's side, two side lockers on passenger's side and one rear locker, all with roller shutter doors

Dimensions: Height 9 ft 8 in, Weight: UW 3 tons 14 cwt, LW 5 tons 10 cwt, Length 20 ft, Breadth 7 ft

The Glasgow Corps stressed the training of personnel and divided it into the following groups:

a. Care and maintenance of all mechanical equipment such as pumps, generators, suction drying machines, smoke deodorisers, smoke extraction fans, etc.

b. All aspects of health and safety including the use of breathing apparatus equipment, ladders and a knowledge of building construction.

c. The proper use and application of salvage sheets, roofing tarpaulins and the general requirements of fire salvage.

Part of the comprehensive equipment carried on the Glasgow Damage Control units in the early 1980s.

The Corps enjoyed close co-operation with Strathclyde Fire Brigade, having a direct line to their Control Room. There was an immediate Turn-out to all calls in Glasgow Central Area and to special risks of hospitals, museums, art galleries and buildings of historic interest, the Corps receiving some 14,800 calls a year. Incidents in the outer areas of the city were attended at the discretion of the Duty Officer, and in the early 1980s Glasgow Corps adopted a deliberate policy of non-attendance at automatic fire alarms until a message confirming a fire was received. The Chief Salvage Officer in part attributed the drop in attendances for 1981 by 576 on the 2,283 in 1980 to this decision.

One of the Leyland appliances purchased by London Salvage Corps during 1923.

This war-surplus Austin ATV was acquired by the London Corps in 1946. The rear part of the body section was re-built during 1960 by the Corps Workshop and the vehicle remained in service until 1963.

LONDON SALVAGE CORPS

Making its début in 1866, the London Salvage Corps initially had Peter Swanton as its Chief Officer, a man with 18 years' experience as a fireman. The headquarters in Watling Street was supported by three out stations, with personnel being a mixture of whole-time staff plus auxiliaries who were called on when required. The Corps moved to the Aldersgate premises in 1961.

In the early days, London Salvage Corps employed horse-drawn carriages which continued in service until 1923 when several motorised Leyland tenders were received, later appliances including Austin ATVs and Morris appliances.

During World War One, the London Salvage Corps put themselves voluntarily at the disposal of the Chief Officer of London Fire Brigade for assistance at air raid fires, while during World War Two the London Corps was again in action fighting fires. They had heavy pump units in addition to salvage tenders and salvagemen made a considerable contribution to both firefighting and salvage work during enemy raids.

Prior to closure in March 1984, the London Salvage Corps received some 46,000 calls a year, attended by these vehicles:

One of the last appliances purchased by the Corps, the Dodge G13/HCB-Angus vehicle received power from a diesel engine.

Type	Make	Model	Fuel	Registration	Registered	Replacement
Salvage Tender	Dodge	K 850	Diesel	ULF 743M	1974	1983
Salvage Tender	Dodge	G 13	Diesel	ALY 911Y	1982	1990
Salvage Tender	Ford	D 1114	Diesel	TYO 470S	1977	1985
Salvage Tender	Ford	D 1114	Diesel	DLA 345T	1978	1986
Salvage Tender	Ford	Transit 35 cwt	Petrol	MLC 629V	1980	1984
Salvage Tender	Ford	Transit 35 cwt	Petrol	MLC 630V	1980	1984
General Purpose Van	Ford	Transit 35 cwt	Diesel	WLX 10S	1978	1984
Personnel Carrier	Ford	Transit 25 cwt	Petrol	RLN 333R	1977	1983
Staff Car	Ford	Granada 2.8GL	Petrol	MLT 999V	1980	1984
Staff Car	Ford	Cortina 2.0GL	Petrol	SLA 333W	1981	1985
Staff Car	Ford	Escort 1.6 GL	Petrol	OLH 345W	1981	1985
Staff Car	Ford	Escort 1.3	Petrol	MLT 278V	1980	1984
Staff Car	Ford	Escort 1.3	Petrol	MLT 581V	1980	1984

Maximum dimensions of largest vehicles
Length (including ladder) 7483 mm
Width 2286 mm
Height 3050 mm

6
Two Examples of Fire Brigades in Britain

In order to present a fuller picture of firefighting in Britain, one could usefully consider particular fire brigades, looking in some detail at such areas as organisation, manning levels, incidents and fleet lists. To accommodate both metropolitan and county authorities, the Brigades of London and Cheshire are described.

LONDON FIRE BRIGADE

INTRODUCTION AND ORGANISATION

Fire-fighting in London has come under the jurisdiction of a number of authorities: the London Fire Engine Establishment between 1833 and 1865, the Metropolitan Fire Brigade between 1866 and 1903 and London Fire Brigade (London County Council) from 1903 until 1941. The Brigade's title was changed to the London Fire Brigade in 1904 by an Act of Parliament, although it had been popularly known as this for some time.

When the National Fire Service appeared in 1941, the separate brigades in Greater London were merged into a single Regional Force eventually divided into four Fire Forces, and, following the end of the World War Two, it was decided that brigades could be organised by counties and County Borough Councils, this taking effect during 1948 when Mr Delve assumed command of London Fire Brigade. He was succeeded by Mr Leete in 1962.

During the following year, 1963, the Greater London Council was recognised as the fire authority for the area previously covered by West Ham, East Ham, Middlesex, London and parts of Kent, Surrey, Hertfordshire and Essex, the new Brigade coming into operation in April 1965 with Mr Leete as CFO. Mr Milner took over from him in 1970, and he in turn was succeeded in 1976 by Mr Darby, who became Her Majesty's Chief Inspector of Fire Services for England and Wales in 1981, his rôle as CFO in London having been taken over by Mr Bullers, formerly CFO for Greater Manchester Fire Service.

London Fire Brigade headquarters is based at Lambeth and there are eleven divisions, 114 fire stations and some 6,900 operational personnel to man over 500 fire appliances which respond to about 108,000 calls per annum. There are about 200 control operators and approximately 880 non-uniformed staff in the Brigade. The 610 square miles of Greater London are divided into three areas with control rooms at Stratford in East London, Croydon in South London and Wembley in North West London. The Brigade moved to central mobilising during 1985, this facilitated by the

largest display unit of its kind, which tells control officers at a glance which appliances are available and which are at incidents in the 114 fire stations.

During 1987, the Brigade is planning to introduce a resource availability system (RAS) which will enable officers in fire appliances to send, via push-button 'data boxes' in cabs, encoded messages for booking mobile and closing down at home station and so on. The messages will be fed via the radio system into the main mobilising computers and wall map which will automatically be kept up to date on vehicle availability.

The Brigade has a policy of fire station rebuilding and replacement when necessary, one of the latest to open being H33 Beckenham, while A24, Soho, was rehoused in modern premises during 1983.

The eleven Divisions at respective stations are as follows:

Divisions

'A' Division HQ—156 Harrow Road, W2 6NL
Stations: A21 Paddington, A22 Manchester Square, A23 Euston, A24 Soho, A25 Westminster, A26 Knightsbridge, A27 Chelsea, A28 Kensington, A29 North Kensington
'B' Division HQ—29 Old Town, SW4 0JT
Stations: B21 Clapham, B22 Lambeth (including river station), B23 Southwark, B24 Dockhead, B26 Old Kent Road, B27 Deptford, B28 Peckham, B29 New Cross, B30 Brixton, B31 West Norwood
'C' Division HQ—235 Old Street, EC1V 9EY
Stations: C21 Shoreditch, C22 Kingsland, C23 Stoke Newington, C24 Whitechapel, C25 Dowgate, C26 Barbican, C27 Clerkenwell, C28 Islington, C29 Kentish Town, C30 Holloway
'D' Division HQ—Marion House, 61–63 Staines Road, Hounslow, TW3 3JQ.
Stations: D21 Ealing, D22 Acton, D23 Hammersmith, D24 Fulham, D25 Chiswick, D26 Twickenham, D27 Heston, D28 Feltham, D29 Southall, D30 Hayes, D31 Hillingdon
'E' Division HQ—249–259 Lewisham High Street, SE13 6NH
Stations: E21 Lewisham, E22 Greenwich, E23 East Greenwich, E24 Woolwich, E25 Plumstead, E26 Shooters Hill, E27 Erith, E28 Bexley, E29 Lee Green, E30 Eltham, E31 Forest Hill, E32 Downham
'F' Division HQ—168 East India Dock Road, E14 0BP
Stations: F21 Stratford, F22 Poplar, F23 Millwall, F25 Shadwell, F26 Bethnal Green, F27 Bow, F28 Homerton, F29 Leyton, F30 Leytonstone
'G' Division HQ—591 Harrow Road, Wembley, HA0 2EC
Stations: G21 Harrow, G22 Stanmore, G23 Mill Hill, G24 Hendon, G25 West Hampstead, G26 Belsize, G28 Willesden, G29 Park Royal, G30 Wembley, G31 Northolt, G32 Ruislip
'H' Division HQ—90 Old Town, Croydon, CR0 1AR
Stations: H21 Bromley, H23 Sidcup, H24 Orpington, H25 Biggin Hill, H26 Addington, H28 Woodside, H29 Purley, H30 Sanderstead, H31 Croydon, H32 Norbury, H33 Beckenham
'J' Division HQ—99 Church Street, N9 9A
Stations; J21 Edmonton, J22 Chingford, J23 Woodford, J24 Walthamstow,

J25 Tottenham, J26 Hornsey, J27 Finchley, J28 Southgate, J29 Barnet, J30 Enfield

'K' Division HQ—Vactric House, 181–191 Garth Road, Morden, SM4 4NF

Stations: K21 Wimbledon, K22 Wandsworth, K23 Battersea, K24 Tooting, K26 Mitcham, K27 Wallington, K28 Sutton, K29 Surbiton, K30 New Malden, K31 Kingston, K32 Richmond

'L' Division HQ—210 High Street South, E6 3RS

Stations: L21 East Ham, L22 Ilford, L23 Hainault, L24 Romford, L25 Dagenham, L26 Hornchurch, L27 Barking, L28 Wennington, L29 Silvertown, L30 Plaistow

Men from Station F21, Stratford, removing chemicals which had fallen from a lorry.

London Fire Brigade personnel from 'E' Division using a water spray to absorb ammonia fumes at Ellis and Everard's chemical plant.

INCIDENTS

In twenty years or so London Fire Brigade has received an increasingly large number of fire calls.

Year	Total calls	Total fires	FB personnel injured at incidents	Adult injuries	Child injuries	Total rescues
0.4 to 12.1965	39,756	21,070	69	553	61	91
1966	55,516	30,436	116	807	189	116
1967	60,254	32,956	97	818	152	177
1968	65,732	32,922	107	866	175	209
1969	75,468	43,733	113	903	205	269
1970	84,538	51,835	98	961	207	220
1971	76,032	42,593	66	814	119	267
1972	87,406	48,159	82	918	165	222
1973	93,167	47,866	87	932	140	297
1974	87,307	46,047	89	954	167	344
1975	93,542	51,539	77	696	73	318
1976	111,520	63,524	117	764	92	464
1977	79,831	36,851	148	496	92	274
1978	95,908	43,433	99	858	134	538
1979	109,467	51,676	163	923	160	684
1980	103,615	46,064	148	683	127	508
1981	103,838	43,793	145	947	140	759

Special Service calls test the skill and expertise of the Brigade.

Incidents are divided into certain categories. If one were to take 1978 as an example, one would find that, of the 95,908 emergency calls received, 43,433 were calls to fires, 703 to chimney fires and 19,828 to special services. False alarms (good intent) amounted to 16,241 and the Brigade had to contend with 15,703 malicious false alarms in 1978. To appreciate fully recent trends, one can usefully study figures for 1982.

INCIDENTS ATTENDED DURING 1982

Fires (excluding chimney)	44,713
Chimney fires	502
False alarms—Due to apparatus	9,006
False alarms—Good intent	7,697
False alarms—Malicious	18,212
Special services	27,677
Total	**107,807**
Make-up fires	
4 pumps	794
6 pumps	81
8 pumps	25
10 pumps	17
12 pumps	3
15 pumps	3
20 pumps	2
25 pumps	—
30 pumps	—
35 and over	—
Total	**925**
Rescues:	
Escape ladder	26
Extension ladder	51
First floor ladder	4
Hook ladder	3
Turntable ladder (including hydraulic platform)	—
Other means	1,150
Total	**1,234**

The resources of the Brigade are tested at major incidents where appliances and personnel are mobilised from a variety of Divisions. One instance during the early 1980s was a fifteen-pump fire which took place in Oxford Street, the Make-Up details taken from '*London Fireman*'.

1139   Called by exchange telephone to fire, 233 Oxford Street, off Great Portland Street, W1. Initial attendance A24 PE, P, A22 P, C24 TL. Further calls at 1158(3) and 1204.

1149   Informative At 233 Oxford Street, W1, basement heavily smoke-logged. BA crews searching.

1153   Make pumps 4. Additional attendance: A22 PE, D28 FOT with Hi-ex foam unit, 'A' Div DCU.

The drama of the Oxford Street fire is captured on this LFB photograph.

1155   Informative: Shop and dwellings five metres by fifteen metres, 25 per cent of basement alight.

1200   Electrical apparatus involved, unable to shut down supply, request urgent attendance of LEB. Urgent attendance of police required to control traffic and public.

1202   Make pumps 6. Additional attendance: A23 P by R/T, A25 P by R/T. TWA informed.

1211   Make pumps 8. Additional attendance: C29 P by R/T, B23P by R/T, A23 ET, D27 ET, J24 HLL, HQ CU, FIT. Ambulance ordered.

1218   Underground tube system affected by smoke, crews investigating. Recommend LT trains pass through station.

1221 Informative: Shop and offices of four floors and basement, five metres by fifteen metres, basement and ground floor alight.

1241 Make pumps 12. Additional attendance: A27 P by R/T, A28 P (from A22), A26 PE by R/T, A25 PE by R/T.

1245 Revised dimensions should read 30 metres by 60 metres.

1253 Make pumps 15. Additional attendance: B21 P by R/T, C27 PE by R/T.

1259 Informative: Two shops and storerooms, four floors and basement, 30 metres by 60 metres, basement and ground floor alight. Very heavy smokelogging.

1301 Salvation Army CaV ordered.

1348 8 pumps, 4 station officers, 1 turntable ladder, 1 divisional control unit required as relief as soon as possible. Ordered: A21 P, D24 P, D22 P, D26 P, G24 P, G28 P, C24 P, B27 P, A24 TL, 'G' Div DCU.

1411 Fire surrounded.

1431 Stop for Oxford Street. Gentlemen's outfitters and storerooms of four floors and basement, 30 metres by 60 metres, all floors and 20 per cent of roof damaged by fire. 7 jets, 1 turntable ladder monitor, BA. Same as all calls.

VEHICLES

The Brigade's appliances including reserve vehicles include the following: 331 Pumping Appliances, eleven Emergency Tenders, seventeen Hydraulic Platforms, fifteen Turntable Ladders, eight Foam Tenders, nine Hose Laying Lorries, two Fire Boats, two Control Units, two Chemical Incident

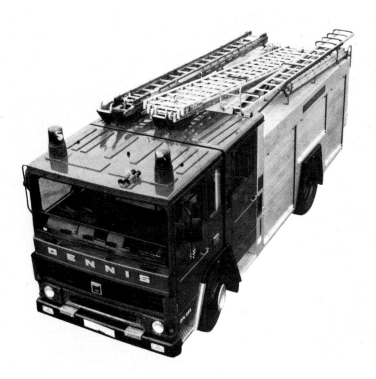

One of the Dennis SS 131 machines acquired in 1983–84.

Units, twelve Divisional Control Unit Pods, one Photographic Unit, one Fire Investigation Unit, 33 Training Appliances and 200 Ancillary Vehicles.

London Fire Brigade has an impressive array of pumping appliances, some referred to as DP machines (Dual Purpose—Pump Escapes or Pumps); DPL appliances (Multi-Purpose—Dewhurst Pump Ladders or Pump Ladders or Pumps) and PL vehicles (Dual Purpose—Pump Ladders or Pumps). Brigade fleet lists change at regular intervals as new machines are acquired. During 1984–85 London Fire Brigade purchased 26 Dennis SS Pump Ladders while 1985 saw the withdrawal of the last operational Wheeled Escape from London Fire Brigade. 1984 saw the end of the traditional Chemical Incident Units in the Brigade, the job now being done by half a dozen Emergency Tenders which had been suitably equipped. About the same time the Canteen Van was withdrawn, its duties taken over by the Salvation Army Unit.

A selection of Pumping Appliances and locations is provided (R–Reserve; T–Training).

For some time London Fire Brigade favoured Merryweather/AEC Turntable Ladders, the mid-1970s bringing a change with Metz Models/ERF, while the Magirus/Dodge/Carmichael machines are a feature of the mid-1980s, exemplified by the TL received in 1985, A805 TYO.

Pictured before delivery in 1980, one of London's Shelvoke and Drewry/CFE machines.

PUMPING APPLIANCES

Make and Type	Registration (Year)	Fleet Number	Use	Location
Dennis F. 109 (Auto)	VAN 500M (1974)	P.500	DP	K.31
Dennis F.109 (Auto)	XYH 510N (1974)	P.510	PL	B.26
ERF 84 PF (UMP Pump) (Auto)	VAN 523M (1974)	P.523	DP	K.27
ERF 84 PF (UMP Pump) (Auto)	GYM 285N (1975)	P.535	DPL	J.23
ERF 84 PF (UMP Pump) (Auto)	OUV 328R (1977)	P.572	DPL	J.27
Dennis F.131 (UMP Pump) (Auto)	UYU 718S (1978)	P.582	DP	A.24
Dennis F.131 (UMP Pump) (Auto)	UYU 719S (1978)	P.583	DP	A.24
CFE/S&D WX (UMP Pump) (Auto)	YHV 203T (1979)	P.603	PL	B.22
CFE/S&D WX (UMP Pump) (Auto)	GYW 614W (1980)	P.614	PL	B.29
CFE/S&D WX (UMP Pump) (Auto)	GYW 625W (1980)	P.625	DP	K.22
CFE/Doge RG 13 (UMP Pump) (Auto)	GYW 633W/658W (1980)	P.633/P.658	PL	E.26 and elsewhere
Dodge RG13/HCB-Angus (UMP Pump) (Auto)	KUV 659X/694X (1982)	P.659/P.694	DPL	J.22 and elsewhere
Dennis SS 131 (UMP Pump) (Auto)	NYV 695Y/735Y (1983)	P.695/P.735	DPL	H.26 and elsewhere

TURNTABLE LADDERS

Make and Type	Registration (Year)	Fleet Number	Use	Location
Merryweather/AEC	CBY 1 (1963)	TL.19*	TL(R)	H.21
Merryweather/AEC	241 FLM (1964)	TL.24P*	TLP(R)	B.24
Merryweather/AEC	CYE 243C (1965)	TL.26P*	TLP	C.24
Merryweather/AEC	CYE 245C (1965)	TL.28P*	TLP(R)	C.21
Merryweather/AEC	CYE 246C (1965)	TL.29P*	TLP(R)	B.24
Merryweather/AEC	EYX 248C (1965)	TL.31P*	TLP(R)	G.24
Merryweather/AEC	JUL 57D (1966)	TL.32P*	TLP(R)	A.27
Merryweather/AEC	JUL 58D (1966)	TL.33P*	TLP	B.31
Merryweather/AEC	JUL 60D (1967)	TL.35P	TLP(T)	T/C
Merryweather/AEC	JUL 61D (1967)	TL.36P	TLP(R)	G.24
Merryweather/AEC	JUL 62D (1966)	TL.37P	TLP(R)	K.21
Metz DL30/ERF 84 PS (Auto)	GYM 268N (1975)	TL.38P	TLP	G.30
Metz DL30/ERF 84 PS (Auto)	OYT 509R (1977)	TL.39P	TLP(R)	A.27
Magirus DL30U/ Dodge (Auto)	NYV 790Y (1983)	TL.40P	TLP	C.24
Magirus DL30U/ Dodge (Auto)	NYV 791Y (1983)	TL.41P	TLP	B.31
Magirus DL30U/ Dodge (Auto)	A792 SUL (1983)	TL.42P	TLP	D.27
Magirus DL30U/ Dodge (Auto)	NYV 793Y (1983)	TL.43P	TLP	H.21
Magirus DL30U/ Dodge (Auto)	NYV 794Y (1983)	TL.44P	TLP	A.24

* For disposal

Based at C24, Whitechapel, the TLP is a Dodge (Auto)/Carmichael/ Magirus DL 30 OU.

An example of a Shelvoke and Drewry/CFE/Simon SS 220 Hydraulic Platform received by London in 1980.

Hydraulic Platforms come in a variety of guises, the ERF 84 PS/Simon SS70 (1973) model based at L30 (TLO 101M), while 1980 heralded the approach of a batch of Shelvoke and Drewry/CFE Simon SS 220 models, more recent marques appearing on Dennis and Dodge chassis.

HYDRAULIC PLATFORMS

Make and Type	Fleet Registration (Year)	Number	Use	Location
Simon SS70/ERF 84 PS (Auto)	TLO 101M (1973)	HP.1P	HPP(R)	L.30
Simon SS70/Dennis F.123 (Auto)	OUV 291R (1977)	HP.2P	HPP(R)	C.21
CFE/S & DWY/Simon SS220 (Auto)	GYW 663W (1980)	HP.3P	HPP(R)	K.28
CFE/S & DWY/Simon SS220 (Auto)	GYW 664W (1980)	HP.4P	HPP(T)	T/C
CFE/S & DWY/Simon SS220 (Auto)	GYW 665W (1980)	HP.5P	HPP(R)	A.27
CFE/S & DWY/Simon SS220 (Auto)	GYW 666W (1980)	HP.6P	HPP	A.28
CFE/S & DWY/Simon SS220 (Auto)	GYW 667W (1980)	HP.7P	HPP	J.25
CFE/S & DWY/Simon SS220 (Auto)	GYW 668W (1980)	HP.8P	HPP	A.21
CFE/S & DWY/Simon SS220 (Auto)	GYW 669W (1980)	HP.9P	HPP	K.22
CFE/S & DWY/Simon SS220 (Auto)	KUV 695X (1981)	HP.10P	HPP	K.31
CFE/S & DWY/Simon SS220 (Auto)	KUV 696X (1981)	HP.11P	HPP	F.22
CFE/S & DWY/Simon SS220 (Auto)	KUV 697X (1981)	HP.12P	HPP	C.22
Dennis/F125 Simon SS220 (Auto)	NYV 773Y (1982)	HP.13P	HPP	L.25
Dennis/F125 Simon SS220 (Auto)	NYV 774Y (1982)	HP.14P	HPP	C.26
Dennis/F125 Simon SS220 (Auto)	NYV 775Y (1982)	HP.15P	HPP	E.22
Dodge/Simon SS220 (Auto)	NYV 736Y (1983)	HP.16P	HPP	H.31
Dodge/Simon SS220 (Auto)	NYV 772Y (1983)	HP.17P	HPP	B.22

London boasts a variety of other specialist machines, some of which are outlined below. Naturally there are several examples of most of each.

OTHER SPECIALIST APPLIANCES

Make and Type	Registration	(Year)	Fleet Number	Motor Fuel	Use	Location
Control Units						
Wadhams/Commer (Walk Thru Chassis)	PAN 6E	(1967)	CU.6	D	CU(R)	Brigade HQ
Ford/Anglo R.1014	OYT 517R	(1977)	CU.7	D	CU	Brigade HQ
Foam Tenders						
Chubb/Unipower R.42 (Auto)	OUV 290R	(1977)	FT.10	D	FT	E.30
Merryweather/Dennis F.131 (Auto)	UYU 730S	(1978)	FT.14	D	FT	L.27
Hose Laying Lorries						
Dodge Commando RG 13 (Chassis Only)	KUV 747X	(1981)	HL.17	D	HL	K.28
Hose Laying Lorry (Demountable Pod)						
Wadham Stringer	GYW 716W		HL.16/1) 16/2)	HL	POD	D.30
Wadham Stringer	KUV 747X		HL.17/3) 17/4)	HL	POD	K.28
Hose Laying Lorry (Demountable Bodies 12)						
Wadham Stringer	—		HLB1		HL	D.30
Photographic Unit						
Ford Cortina Estate	YHV 222T	(1979)	PHO.2	P	PHO	Brigade HQ
Fireboats						
Watercraft, Gross Tonnage 18.74	—	(1975)	*Fire Swift*	Gas Oil	FBt(R)	B.22
Watercraft, Gross Tonnage 18.74	—	(1976)	*Fire Hawk*	Gas Oil	FBt	B.22
A catamaran was ordered for 1985, carrying a 35-foot hydraulic platform.						

Pictured at an incident, the Ford R1014/Anglo Control Unit entered service in 1977.

There are numerous ancillary vehicles such as repair vans, personnel carriers and demountable chassis/cabs. Some examples are:

ANCILLARY VEHICLES

Make and Type	Registration (Year)	Fleet Number	Motor Fuel	Use	Location
Mobile Repair Vans					
Dodge S.56/Hawson	KUV 742X (1982)	MRV.22	D	MRV	Lambeth W/S
Chassis/Cabs—Demountable					
Bedford CF 350L	NYV 776Y/ (1983) 824Y	DC16/ DC54	P	DC	D Div HQ and other Div HQs
Small Demountable Bodies					
General Purpose Vans					
Ray/Smith/ CFE	(1981)	VB1		GP	A Div HQ
Ray/Smith/ Wadham Stringer	(1982)	VB10		GP	TSB BA
Personnel Carriers					
Ray/Smith/ Wadham Stringer	(1982)	PCB1		PC	G Div HQ
Ray/Smith Wadham Stringer	(1983)	PCB8		PC	D Div HQ
Divisional Control Unit Pods	(1983)	DCU1B/ DCU12B		DCU	

PERSONNEL

People wishing to join London Fire Brigade should be aged between 18 and 30 years inclusive, or up to 34 years inclusive for ex-service personnel, and must measure at least 5 ft 6 in (1.68 metres) in height, having good physical qualities too. Would-be recruits undergo a test in dictation, arithmetic and IQ, and, if accepted, carry out a fourteen-week training period at the Brigade's Training Centre at Southwark. Training is carried on within the guidelines of the Home Office Syllabus and two weeks are spent in the mid-part of the course on Breathing Apparatus (BA), allowing personnel, after qualifying in BA, to experience work on ladders and so on. Recruits are monitored throughout the course and instructors hold a weekly quiz on each squad to test acquisition of facts. Recruits undergo a series of further tests set by the Course Director. Standards are high at Southwark, so that fire personnel who have followed the fourteen-week full-time course will be able to work in confidence alongside professional colleagues in one of the Brigade's many stations. Interestingly, London Fire Brigade had four full-time female firefighters on operational work during 1985, working alongside male colleagues.

CHESHIRE FIRE BRIGADE

INTRODUCTION AND ORGANISATION

Cheshire Fire Brigade was formed during 1974, as a result of reorganisation, from the brigades of Cheshire County, Chester City, Lancashire County and Warrington Borough. The present Chief Fire Officer is Mr A.N. Lightbody, OBE, QFSM, FIFireE. Cheshire Fire Brigade is an example of a modern organisation employing the latest techniques and skills in fire-fighting and general brigade procedures, the fleet, fire stations and equipment being second to none in the United Kingdom.

Cheshire is a county of outstanding beauty, much of the surface comprising an extensive level plain between the Welsh and Derbyshire mountains. The north eastern sector of the county offers impressive hill scenery, bordering on the Peak District, where one finds pleasantly situated towns and villages such as Poynton and Macclesfield.

Providing fire cover for some 930,000 inhabitants, the Cheshire Fire Brigade covers an area of 897 square miles, taking in both urban and rural districts. The Brigade's 24 fire stations are staffed by whole-time and retained personnel, with certain stations relying entirely on retained firemen

Retained and wholetime firemen tackle a Cheshire mill fire during the late 1970s.

142

and some having both whole-time and retained, while Warrington and Birchwood are manned solely by whole-time personnel. The authorised strength is 690 whole-time and 328 retained staff, and, for the purposes of administration, the Brigade is split into three Divisions, each with a Divisional HQ, at Chester ('A' Division), Warrington ('B' Division) and Crewe ('C' Division); the Brigade HQ is also located at Chester.

INCIDENTS

A large Brigade such as Cheshire has a variety of incidents ranging from special service calls to mill fires and chemical incidents attended by retained and whole-time personnel alike. The approximate number of jobs per year are as follows: 'A' Division has seven fire stations and receives 3,152 calls; 'B' Division has six fire stations and receives 3,521 calls; and 'C' Division has eleven fire stations and receives 2,456 calls. The total calls received in Cheshire for one year (1982) numbered 9,129, with 24,102 appliance movements. In addition, there were 322 calls for assistance to neighbouring brigades. If one were to consider principal fires in recent times, one need look no further than the incidents in 1984 at a Warrington timber importers and an Ellesmere Port paper manufacturers, the fires causing considerable damage. The Warrington one alone costing £3 million to replace stock and premises, while the paper mill incident lasted several days in the spring, both jobs requiring the attendance of crews from all divisions of Cheshire Fire Brigade.

To appreciate further the task of Cheshire Fire personnel one can examine a specific incident which underlines the first-class mobilising and fire-fighting operations within the county. On 3 March 1983 a petrol tanker train came off the rails at Bellhouse Lane near Stockton Heath, subsequent

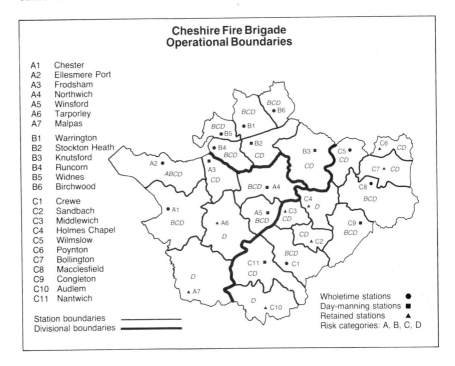

Cheshire Fire Brigade Operational Boundaries

A1 Chester
A2 Ellesmere Port
A3 Frodsham
A4 Northwich
A5 Winsford
A6 Tarporley
A7 Malpas

B1 Warrington
B2 Stockton Heath
B3 Knutsford
B4 Runcorn
B5 Widnes
B6 Birchwood

C1 Crewe
C2 Sandbach
C3 Middlewich
C4 Holmes Chapel
C5 Wilmslow
C6 Poynton
C7 Bollington
C8 Macclesfield
C9 Congleton
C10 Audlem
C11 Nantwich

Station boundaries ——————
Divisional boundaries ——————

Wholetime stations ●
Day-manning stations ■
Retained stations ▲
Risk categories: A, B, C, D

143

investigations revealing that the derailed goods train was carrying 350 tonnes of Gas Oil and had demolished an overhead 25 Kv power line, causing live cables to fall and short circuit on steel work of tank waggons, this in turn igniting spilled gas oil. Crews arriving on the scene were met with dense smoke, flame, derailed tankers and a tangled mass of overhead gantries and cables. The messages and times tell the story:

Cheshire fire personnel battling with the gas oil blaze near Stockton Heath.

0715 First call received—the attendance was: B21 (Stockton Heath), B41 (Runcorn), B42 (Runcorn), B11 (Warrington), Foam Tender B18 (Warrington), Emergency Tender B59 (Widnes), L4V from A4 (Northwich) and B3 (Knutsford).

0723 Make Pumps 10—Machines attending were B12 (Warrington), B51 (Widnes), A41 (Northwich), A31 (Frodsham), A21 (Ellesmere Port), Emergency Tender A19 (Chester), Control Unit A15 (Chester), Petrol Carrier C1 (Crewe), Canteen Van A4 (Northwich).

0726 In Attendance (B21, Stockton Heath).

0726 Isolate overhead power stanchion 2590 m (confirmed 0731).

0728 First informative message—From Sub Officer Webster—'Incident involving derailed train approximately 8 rail tankers containing gas kerosene well alight.'

0733 Rail Tank Explosion—Crews withdrawn (a ball of flame was sent over the head of crews and a large area of the fireground).

0754 From Divisional Officer Davis—'Serious fire involving train petrol tankers. Relays being established.'

(The nearest water supply to the incident was the Manchester Ship Canal, but access for fire-fighting purposes was impossible. The alternative supply was a canal about one mile away, this providing a twinned-water relay.)

0809 Water Relay completed. One Jetmaster in use.

0858 From County Fire Officer—'Make Pumps 15 for hose supplies. Second relay completed.' Machines attending Make Pumps 15 were B61 (Birchwood), A22 (Ellesmere Port), A23 (Ellesmere Port), B13, (Warrington), B52 (Widnes), Pump Merseyside.

0931 From County Fire Officer—'Fire now knocked down. Three tanks ruptured and on fire.'

0942 From County Fire Officer—Stop.

1217 Divisional Commander Davis, 'British Rail recovery operations to commence in 30 minutes. Pumps reduced to 5.'

1330 DO Mackintosh—'Six line relay reduced to 4.'

1456 BR have cranes in attendance.

(Recovery operations were continued through the night, the relay reduced to two lines and 5 crews stood by until 09.35 hours, 4th March, 1983. 4 March 1983.)

1020 BR Recovery Operation complete. Making up in progress.

1210 Divisional Officer Moyle—'Incident now closed.'

This incident serves to highlight the efficiency of Cheshire Fire Brigade and, at a public enquiry held in Crewe, the Fire Service was praised for their efforts and determination. Some 4,300 litres of foam compound and 540,000 gallons of water were employed in the job by 106 fire personnel, and 230 tonnes of gas oil were destroyed by fire. Four 32 tonne and one 100 tonne

capacity tank waggons were severely damaged by fire while extensive heat damage was apparent with three 32 tonne capacity tank waggons and 1,000 m² of grassland destroyed.

VEHICLES

A consideration of Cheshire's fleet list in 1962/62 indicates the variety of appliances owned by many county brigades some 25 years ago when the following vehicles and appliances were in use in the Brigade:

Category	Quantity
Pump Escapes	10
Water Tender Escape	1
Pump 30/35-ft Extension Ladder	1
Water Tender 30/35-ft Extension Ladders	34
Water Tender 45-ft Extension Ladders	5
Pump Salvage Tender	1
Foam Tenders	4
Hose Laying Lorry	1
Turntable Ladders	3
Hose Reel Tenders	5
Towing Vehicle	1
General Purpose Vehicles	6
Passenger Carrier	1
Service Vans	3
Stack Drag	1
Breakdown Lorry	1
Light Four-Wheel Drive Vehicles (Land Rovers)	12
Utility Vans	21
Staff Cars	49
Large Trailer Pumps	12
Light Trailer Pumps	12
Wheelbarrow Pump	1
Light Portable Pumps carried on Water Tenders and Land Rovers	61
Total	246

NEW APPLIANCES RECEIVED DURING 1961/62

Vehicle	Ordered	Allocation
Two Dennis Type F.24 Appliances:		
Water Tender Escape	April 1961	A.2 Stalybridge
Water Tender 45-ft Extension Ladder	April 1961	B.4 Altrincham
Dennis Type F.28 Appliance:		
Water Tender 30/35 ft. Extension Ladder	April 1961	A.3 Cheadle Hulme
One Foam Tender	August 1961	B.4 Altrincham

The following new vehicles, etc. were also received during 1961/62: three Land Rovers; one General Purpose Lorry; one A.35 Austin Utility Vehicle; seven Coventry Climax Lightweight Pumps; seven Alcon Pumps; two Hillman Saloon Cars; six Hillman Huskies; six Morris Minor Cars; and one Morris Mini Minor Car. A Water Tender was converted to a General Purpose Lorry.

New in the early 1960s, this Dennis F38/Dennis Water Tender was sold in 1982, finishing its days as a spare appliance.

The following obsolete appliances, vehicles, etc., were disposed of during 1961/62: four Pump Escapes; five Self Propelled Pumps; one Water Tender; one Large Trailer Pump; seven Light Trailer Pumps; four Light Pumps; two Towing Vehicles; five Wheelbarrow Pumps; three General Purpose Vehicles; three Utility Vans (including 1 written-off after accident damage); six Staff Cars; and one Merryweather Escape

Auxiliary Fire Service Appliances

During the year, one futher Pump/Water Tender and two motor cycles were received from the Home Office on loan for Auxiliary Fire Service training, and two Austin Towing vehicles, four large trailer pumps and four light trailer pumps were returned to the Home Office as surplus to requirements. The fleet was made up of 21 vehicles as follows: eight Pump Water Tenders; two Towing Vehicles; one Canteen Van; one Water Transportation Unit (Bikini); one Control Unit; two Command Cars; two Vans; and four Motor Cycles.

The current fleet list can be considered to be one of the most up-to-date in the country:

'A' DIVISION

Category	Make	Registration (Year)
AI Chester		
WrL	Dennis RS 133 (Diesel)	SDM 859V (1980)
	Dennis F108 (Diesel)	UFM 379K (1972)
HP	Dennis F108 50 ft PHP Manual (Diesel)	LFM 673J (1971)
	Dennis F125 SS263 Auto/Diesel	WFM 465W (1980)
CU	Bedford KEL/RRB61 Manual	TMB 502R (1976)
ET	Dennis F49 Automatic Onan No. 1	HDM 743N (1975)
BAT	Ford 'A' Series	DTU 346S (1978)
PCV	Bedford CF 250	GOP 682W (1980)
Van	Bedford HA130	JBF 721V (1979)
	Bedford HA130	UFA 376X (1981)
	Bedford CF	DVT 350T (1978)
[Two Hestair Dennis RS 133 WrLs received in 1985]		
A2 Ellesmere Port		
WrL	Dennis RS 133 (Diesel)	SDM 558V (1980)
	ERF 84 RF Automatic	TCA 863R (1976)
	Dennis F49 Automatic	XMB 497M (1974)
HP	ERF 84 RS 70 ft HP Manual	JMB 350G (1969)
FoT	Dennis Delta II Manual/Diesel	EFM 562S (1978)
Vans	Dodge 50 Series	EMA 949X (1981)
	Bedford HA 130	UFA 379X (1981)
[One Hestair Dennis RS 133 WrL received in 1985]		
A3 Frodsham		
WrL	Dennis R61 Automatic	DMB 70S (1978)
	Dennis R61 Automatic	DMB 71S (1978)
[One Hestair Dennis RS 133 WrL received 1985]		
A4 Northwich		
WrL	Dennis RS 133 (Diesel)	HFM 710X (1982)
	ERF 84 RF Automatic	TCA 864R (1976)
L4T	Land Rover (6-Cyl)	DDM 337S (1978)
Van	Bedford HA 130	JBF 722V (1979)
CaV	Ford Transit	YTU 184M (1974)
A5 Winsford		
WrL	Dennis RS 133 (Diesel)	SDM 860V (1980)
	Dennis F45	VLG 789J (1970)
ST	Ford 'A' Series (Diesel)	DTU 347S (1978)
Van	Bedford HA 130	JBF 724V (1980)
A6 Tarporley		
WrL	Dennis 'D' Jaguar XK Engine	CLG 103K (1971)
L4P	Land Rover/Carmichael Redwing	VFM 729R (1977)
A7 Malpas		
WrL	Dennis R61 Automatic	EFM 563S (1978)
L4T	Land Rover Safari V8	DMB 908X (1981)

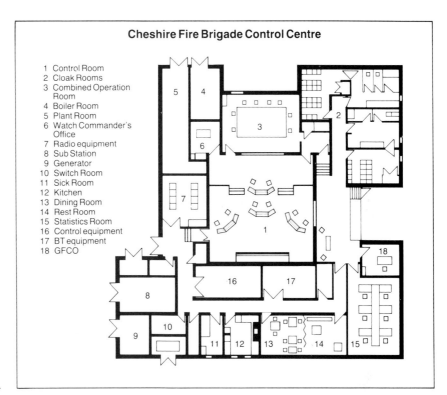

Cheshire Fire Brigade Control Centre

1 Control Room
2 Cloak Rooms
3 Combined Operation Room
4 Boiler Room
5 Plant Room
6 Watch Commander's Office
7 Radio equipment
8 Sub Station
9 Generator
10 Switch Room
11 Sick Room
12 Kitchen
13 Dining Room
14 Rest Room
15 Statistics Room
16 Control equipment
17 BT equipment
18 GFCO

The Chester-based Control Unit TMB 502R is pictured at an incident alongside Crewe's Dennis F61 Emergency Tender.

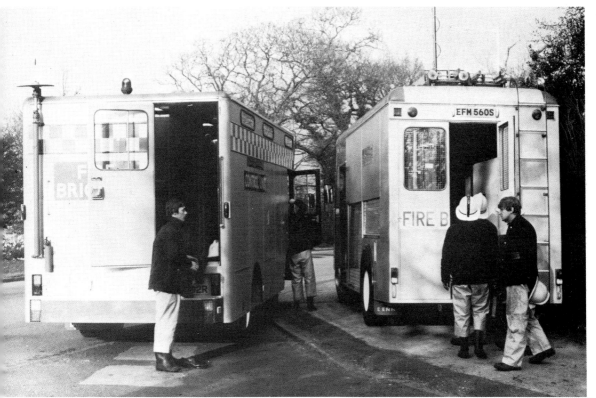

'B' DIVISION

B1 Warrington

WrL	Dennis RS 133 (Diesel)	SDM 557V	(1980)
	Dennis RS 133 (Diesel)	HFM 712X	(1982)
HP	ERF 84 RFS 50 ft PHP Automatic	NMA 397P	(1975)
TL	Bedford/Merryweather 100-ft	WMB 700E	(1967)
FoT	Dennis Delta II. Manual Diesel	EFM 561S	(1978)
PCV	Bedford CF 280	ARF 869Y	(1982)
Vans	Bedford CF	A314 RFM	(1983)
	Bedford HA 130	UFA 378X	(1981)
	Bedford HA 130 (workshop)	JBF 723V	(1980)

[A Dennis/Magirus 100-ft TL delivered in 1985 replaced WMB 700E.]

B2 Stockton Heath

WrL	Dennis R61 Automatic (Low Height)	VCA 493R	(1977)
WrT	Dennis F 38	WMA 314E	(1967)

[Replaced by Hestair Dennis 'DS' WrT in 1985 with 500 gpm UMPX 50 pump.]

Vans	Bedford CF	LEH 114V	(1980)
	Bedford HA 130	YVT 369Y	(1982)

B3 Knutsford

WrL	Dennis RS 133 (Diesel)	EMA 951X	(1982)
L4T	Land Rover Safari V8	DMB 903X	(1981)
RT	Range Rover/Carmichael Commando	DMB 68S	(1978)

B4 Runcorn

WrL	Dennis RS 133 (Diesel)	EMA 950X	(1982)
	ERF 84 RF (Automatic)	TCA 862R	(1976)
L4V	Bedford CF 250 4 × 4	XFA 44X	(1982)
CIU	Ford 'A' Series (Diesel)	SMB 670R	(1976)
Van	Bedford HA 130	EBF 385Y	(1983)

[One Hestair Dennis RS 133 WrL received 1985]

B5 Widnes

WrL	Dennis RS 133 (Diesel)	HFM 709X	(1982)
	Dennis RS 133 (Diesel)	SDM 556V	(1980)
ET	Dennis F61 Automatic Onan No. 4	VTU 433R	(1977)
Van	Bedford HA 130	YVT 370Y	(1982)

B6 Birchwood

WrL	Dennis RS 133 (Diesel)	WFM 466W	(1980)
RT	Range Rover Carmichael Commando	DMB 67S	(1978)
L4T	Land Rover 6-Cyl.	ECA 66S	(1978)
Van	Bedford HA 130	NEH 756W	(1980)

'C' DIVISION

Cl Crewe

WrL	Dennis RS 133 (Diesel)	HFM 711X	(1982)
	ERF 84 RF	TCA 861R	(1976)

L4V	Land Rover (6 Cyl.)	DDM 336S	(1978)
ET	Dennis F61 Automatic Onan NO. 3	EFM 560S	(1978)
Pet C	Bedford CF 250	A320 RFM	(1983)
PCV	Bedford CF 250	DBF 106T	(1978)
Vans	Dodge 50 (Service Van)	XFM 799W	(1980)
	Bedford CF	TVT 183Y	(1981)
	Bedford HA 130	NEH 751W	(1980)

C2 Sandbach

| WrL | Dennis F45 | WLG 317J | (1970) |
| L4T | Land Rover Safari V8 | DMB 902X | (1981) |

C3 Middlewich

| WrL | Dennis F 48 | CMB 770K | (1971) |
| L4P | Land Rover/Carmichael Redwing | NMB 39P | (1975) |

C4 Holmes Chapel

| WrL | Dennis F 45 | VLG 788J | (1970) |
| L4T | Land Rover Safari V8 | DMB 904X | (1981) |

C5 Wilmslow

WrL	Dennis RS 133 (Diesel)	HFM 708X	(1982)
	Dennis F48	CLG 772K	(1971)
L4T	Land Rover 6-Cyl.	ECA 65S	(1978)
Van	Bedford HA 130	NEH 752W	(1980)

C6 Poynton

| WrL | Dennis R61 (Automatic) | DMB 69S | (1978) |
| L4T | Land Rover Safari V8 | DMB 906X | (1981) |

C7 Bollington

| WrL | Dennis R61 (Automatic) | UMA 286R | (1976) |
| L4T | Land Rover Safari V8 | DMB 907X | (1981) |

C8 Macclesfield

WrL	Dennis RS 133 (Diesel)	EMA 948X	(1982)
	Dennis F 49 (Automatic)	PMA 208L	(1973)
HP	Dennis F125/SS 263/Auto-Diesel	WFM 464W	(1980)
L4T	Land Rover Safari V8	DMB 905X	(1981)
Van	Bedford HA 130	YVT 371Y	(1982)

C9 Congleton

WrL	Dennis RS 61 (Automatic)	DMB 72S	(1978)
	Dennis F 48	VLG 787J	(1970)
CIU	Ford 'A' Series	DTU 349S	(1978)
Van	Bedford HA 130	CVT 132T	(1978)

C10 Audlem

| WrL | Dennis R61 Automatic | UMA 287R | (1976) |
| L4T | Land Rover Safari V8 | DMB 901X | (1981) |

C11 Nantwich

| WrL | Dennis R61 Automatic (Low Height) | VCA 494R | (1977) |
| | Dennis F38 | ULG 997E | (1967) |

[Replaced 1984/85 by Hestair Dennis DS WrT]

| Van | Bedford HA 130 | EBF 384Y | (1983) |

The Emergency Tender (left) is a Dennis F61 from Widnes, attending a major job at which Warrington's ERF Hydraulic Platform was present (NMA 397P).

This Dennis RS 133 was one of several received in 1980.

Several 'C' Division Stations, including Poynton, Congleton and Crewe, attended this factory fire in Macclesfield. The Dennis F125 Hydraulic Platform is based at C8 Macclesfield, while the Northwich Water Ladder coming on relief duties (HFM 710X) is a Dennis RS 133.

Rear view of one of the Land Rover 'Safari' V8 appliances (1981), with the portable pump pulled out on its tray.

	'A' Division		
WrLs, WrTs, WrL	ERF 84 RF (Automatic)	FLG 647K	(1972)
	ERF 84 RF (Automatic)	KMA 152L	(1972)
	'B' Division		
	Dennis F 49 (Automatic)	PMA 209L	(1973)
	ERF 84 RF (Automatic)	NED 832M	(1974)
	'C' Division		
	ERF 84 RF (Automatic)	FLG 649K	(1972)
	Dennis F 45	VLG 786J	(1970)
	Workshop		
	ERF 84 RF (Automatic)	CTU 542N	(1974)
L4P	Land Rover/Carmichael Redwing	RTU 894H	(1970)
	Driving School/Training:		
	Dennis F 45	JTU 775G	(1969)
	Dennis F 38	MTU 317H	(1969)
	Dennis F 38	RLG 889H	(1969)
	Dennis F 38	MTU 318H	(1969)
	Dennis F 38	WMA 315E	(1967)
	Bedford CF	YUT 368Y	(1982)

[MTU 318H and WMA 315E were sold in 1985.]

Other Vehicles			
Recovery Vehicle	Bedford M, 4 × 4 Diesel	CLG 510S	(1978)
GPL	Dodge 50 Series (S75)	A720 HBA	(1984)
Stores Van	Ford 'A' Series (Diesel)	DTU 348S	(1978)
Service Vans	Ford 'A' Series Diesel	UCA 788V	(1980)
	Land Rover	UCA 789V	(1980)

[Vehicles to be sold in 1984/85 include the Bedford/Merryweather 100-ft Turntable Ladder WMB 700E from B1 and WrLs RLG 889H, JTU 775G and WrTs ULG 997E, WMA 314/315E and MTU 318H.]

MOBILISING SYSTEM

Cheshire Fire Brigade's microprocessor-based control system epitomises the modern equipment found within the authority. Employing the very latest technology, the system became fully operational in mid-1984, one interesting aspect being the absence of moving parts to be worn out and, consequently, there is no need for routine maintenance. Accommodated in purpose-built premises at Boughton, Chester, the system provides fully centralised control over the Brigade; the building houses a centrally situated control room surrounded by ancillary rooms.

The control room has four consoles, three mobilising positions and a supervisor position. All consoles are independent, and a failure on one position has no effect at any other. There are two operators per mobilising control and, on receipt of a call, information from the caller is recorded under six headings:Caller's Indentity; Incident Type; Address; Risk; Parish; and Additional Information.

Each fire station is linked to Brigade Control by a British Telecom private wire (with PSTN back-up), and the Station's Equipment Box controls

A part of the new Control Centre, opened in 1984.

station lights and bells, alerters, printers and station console, this last piece of equipment allowing direct communication between the station and control or other stations via a private wire.

On receipt of a call, the Control Operator will press the 'Send' button to mobilise appliances. The microprocessor equipment will read the operator's input to discover which appliances are to be sent and which stations are to be alterted. Turnout instructions are then coded and sent to respective stations along with coded commands which activate station bells, lights or alerters ('bleepers').

The turnout message appears on the fire station printer and when the acknowledgement button is pressed, this will register at control on the originating console.

A typical turnout message would read:

Caller's Indentity:	Ches. 673922
Incident Type:	House
Address:	40 James Street
Risk:	
Parish:	Eaton, Chester
Additional Information:	Chip Pan
Mobilising Appliances:	A11, A12
Incident No.:	15437

Details of incidents (points) are recorded in the Incident Summary Book prior to being passed to Brigade Control.

ACKNOWLEDGEMENTS

Many of the photographs were taken by the author, others coming from the John Creighton Collection. The author would like to thank colleagues who assisted further with material, especially the Chief Fire Officers whose Brigades are mentioned in the book. The photograph on the front of the dust jacket was provided by Amoco UK Ltd, to whom gratitude is extended. The photograph on the back, 'Incident in Cheshire', is from the John Creighton Collection.

ABBREVIATIONS

WrL	Water Ladder
WrT	Water Tender
HP	Hydraulic Platform
TL	Turntable Ladder
ET	Emergency Tender
CU	Control Unit
CIU	Chemical Incident Unit
RT	Rescue Tender
BAT	Breathing Apparatus Tender
PCV	Personnel Carrying Vehicle
FoT	Foam Tender
ST	Salvage Tender
CaV	Canteen Van
Pet C	Petrol Carrier
L4T	Light four wheel drive vehicle with hose reel
L4P	Light four-wheel drive with pump

Index